# Yachtmaster

## An Examination Handbook

**By the same authors:**

YACHTMASTER EXERCISES
0 229 11715 5

A companion volume to this book, packed with practice exercises and answers, including over 50 model plots. It comes complete with Admiralty Practice Chart No 5055.

OCEAN YACHTMASTER
Celestial Navigation: An instructional handbook with exercises.
0 229 11695 7

The ideal textbook for the Yachtmaster Ocean Certificate (RYA/DoT), it covers the full range of sight reduction methods and planning ocean passages.

OCEAN YACHTMASTER EXERCISES
Exercises in Celestial Navigation
0 229 11792 9

A companion volume to *Ocean Yachtmaster* for those taking the Yachtmaster Ocean Certificate and for navigators' revision.

COMPETENT CREW/DAY SKIPPER
A companion to the RYA Course
0 229 11736 8

For the novice who is totally unfamiliar with boats, sailing and the sea. The subjects are explained from first principles with diagrams and glossary. Based on the RYA Competent Crew and Day Skipper shorebased and practical courses.

VHF YACHTMASTER
0 229 11720 1

A textbook and accompanying cassette which teach radio communication skills. Includes all information necessary for passing the examination and a question and answer page for revision.

# Yachtmaster

## An Examination Handbook

### Revised and Updated

Pat Langley-Price and Philip Ouvry

**ADLARD COLES**
8 Grafton Street, London W1

Adlard Coles
William Collins Sons & Co. Ltd
8 Grafton Street, London W1X 3LA

First published in Great Britain by
Adlard Coles Ltd 1982
Reprinted 1983, 1984, 1985 (twice)
First edition revised 1987
Reprinted 1988

Distributed in the United States of America
by Sheridan House, Inc.

*British Library Cataloguing in Publication Data*
Langley-Price, Pat
   Yachtmaster: an examination handbook
   with exercises. – Rev. and updated
   1. Yachts and yachting  2. Seamanship
   I. Title     II. Ouvry, Philip
   623.88'223       GV813

ISBN 0 229 11662 0

Printed and bound in Great Britain by
Mackays of Chatham Ltd

# Foreword

When it comes to facing up to the elements at sea, theoretical knowledge – as the authors rightly recognise – is no substitute for practical experience. But there is no doubt whatever that aspiring Yachtmasters or skippers can be very much better prepared if as much as possible is learnt before taking full responsibility for the safety of themselves and others.

In this country we continue to rely primarily on education, in preference to legislation, in establishing standards of competence in the handling of privately owned craft, and this is where the RYA Yachtmaster scheme, which has the full approval and support of the Department of Transport and its Coastguard operational arm, is of vital importance.

Pat Langley-Price and Philip Ouvry will have good cause for personal satisfaction if the study of their very comprehensive handbook contributes, as I'm sure it will, to making sailing not only a pleasure, as it should be, but also a safer pursuit for all those who wish to participate now and in future.

Commander J T Fetherston-Dilke
Chief Coastguard

# Author's note

Practice chart 5055 has now been reprinted and revised. This does not affect the majority of the examples and problems in the book, which can be completed by reference to the portion of chart 5055 printed inside the book jacket.

Students using the revised chart should note the following:

1. The position of the compass rose used in the example on page 29 has changed.

2. Variation is now 5°05'W (1981) decreasing about 8' annually.

3. The tower in Bexhill (question A8, page 175) which is in position 50 50'.7N 0 28'.9E is no longer shown.

# Contents

# Acknowledgements

We have received much valuable help and advice from organisations and friends too numerous to list in full; however, we would like to express our particular gratitude to the following for permission to use their material:

*The International Maritime Organisation.* Extracts from the Convention on the International Regulations for Preventing Collisions at Sea 1972.

*Ministry of Defence, Hydrographic Dept.* Extracts from Admirality Tide Tables, Tidal Stream Atlas and Practice Chart 5055, with the sanction of the controller, HM Stationery Office and of the Hydrographer of the Navy.

*The Royal Yachting Association.* Extracts from G.15 Log book.

*Thomas Reed Publications Ltd.*

*Barnacle Marine Ltd.*

*Imray, Laurie, Norie and Wilson Ltd.*

*APT Electronics Ltd, Beaufort Air Sea Equipment Ltd, Seafarer Navigation International Ltd, Henry Browne & Son Ltd, Bruce Anchors Ltd, Thos Walker & Sons Ltd.* Photographs.

# Introduction

Every boat must have somebody in charge. It is that person's responsibility to ensure that the vessel and crew are capable of standing up to the conditions likely to be encountered on the passage being undertaken. This requirement has been highlighted by the increase in sailing generally, and by the temptation to go further afield which is held out by an expanding array of electronic aids to navigation; from time to time there is unwelcome publicity through disasters in one form or another.

Some countries impose official regulations on where a particular pleasure craft may go, depending on boat, gear and qualification of the skipper. Britain has not yet invoked legal restrictions, but for some time there has been a number of voluntary schemes, each aimed at raising the skill of the yachtsman. In the forefront of the organisations concerned has always been the Royal Yachting Association, and some time ago various other bodies such as the Armed Services, the Sail Training Association and the Ocean Youth Club each brought their training syllabus into line. The result is the RYA/DoT Yachtmaster scheme which, as its title implies, has the approval of the Department of Transport. There are various categories which a person may achieve, and each implies a standard of skill and knowledge and, equally important, a level of experience. These categories are:

1. Competent Crew.
2. Day Skipper/Watch Leader.
3. Coastal Skipper and Yachtmaster Offshore.
4. Yachtmaster Ocean.

Full details of the training scheme are contained in the RYA Cruising Proficiency Syllabus and Logbook for Courses and Certificates of Competence (G.15 Sail, G18 Motor). Extracts are shown on the next two pages.

**OVERALL SCHEME OF CRUISING COURSES AND QUALIFICATIONS**
G15 SAIL

| Grade | Shorebased | Practical Course | Seatime | Examination |
|---|---|---|---|---|
| **RYA Competent Crew** | Combined course for both grades, seamanship and navigation | 5 days. Mainly seamanship and sailing | 5 days 100 miles 4 night hours | None. Completion certificates awarded on satisfactory completion of courses. |
| **RYA Day Skipper/Watch Leader** | | 5 days. Seamanship, sailing and navigation. | 10 days 200 miles 8 night hours | None. Completion certificates awarded on satisfactory completion of courses. |
| **RYA/DoT Coastal Skipper** | Combined course for both grades, navigation and meteorology. | 5 day course on practical skippering | 20 days 400 miles 12 night hours | Oral for holders of shorebased and practical course completion certs. Practical for others. |
| **RYA/DoT Yachtmaster Offshore** | | None | 50 days 2,500 miles 5 passages over 60 miles, 2 as skipper and 2 overnight passages. | Practical Examination |
| **RYA/DoT Yachtmaster Ocean** | Astro navigation and world-wide meteorology | None | Ocean Passage | Open only to Yachtmasters Offshore. Assessment of sights taken at sea + written exam if shore-based proficiency certificate not held |

Our aim is to provide the information required for the shorebased section of the Coastal Skipper and Yachtmaster Offshore Certificate. The book has been written so that a student can either use it as a course manual or for independent study. The supplement based on the Competent Crew and Day Skipper grades will help the keen crew member to learn elementary seamanship.

Whilst this manual is not a substitute for almanacs, pilot books, tide tables, charts etc, it does serve as an introduction to all these publications and is, therefore, not only an important adjunct to any shorebased RYA course, but highly desirable to have on board any seagoing small boat. It is not, however, restricted to candidates for certificates, and the contents have been written so that anyone interested in navigating a sailing or motor boat can learn the skills necessary to go to sea safely, confidently and enjoyably. There is, of course, no substitute for practical experience, so any shorebased course should be followed up with a practical course at a nationally recognised sailing school.

**G18 MOTOR**

| Grade | Shorebased | Practical Course | Seatime | Examination |
|---|---|---|---|---|
| **Introduction to Motor Cruising** | Introductory Shorebased Course | — | — | None. Course completion certificates awarded on satisfactory completion of course. |
| **RYA Competent Crew (Motor)** | Combined course for both grades, seamanship and navigation. | 2 days. Seamanship and boat handling. | 5 days 100 miles | None. Completion certificates awarded on satisfactory completion of courses. |
| **RYA Day Skipper (Motor)** | | 5 days. Seamanship, boat handling and navigation. | 10 days 200 miles 4 night hours | None. Completion certificates awarded on satisfactory completion of courses. |
| **NATIONAL MOTOR CRUISING CERTIFICATE – Awarded to holders of course completion certificates, shorebased and practical, for Day Skipper.** | | | | |
| **RYA/DTp Coastal Skipper (Motor)** | Combined course for both grades, navigation and meteorology. | 5 day course on practical skippering | 20 days 400 miles 12 night hours | Oral for holders of shorebased and practical course completion certs. Practical for others. |
| **RYA/DTp Yachtmaster Offshore (Motor)** | | None | 50 days 2,500 miles 5 passages over 60 miles, 2 as skipper and 2 overnight passages. | Practical Examination |
| **RYA/DTp Yachtmaster Ocean (Motor)** | Astro navigation and world-wide meteorology | None | Ocean Passage | Open only to Yachtmasters Offshore. Assessment of sights taken at sea + written exam if shorebased proficiency certificate not held |

The syllabus for both the Competent Crew/Day Skipper and for the Coastal Skipper/Yachtmaster Offshore shorebased certificates are included at the back of the manual with page references.

An extract from Practice Chart 5055 is reproduced in black and white on the inside of the dust jacket of this book, with kind permission of the Hydrographer. Most of the exercises in the book can be worked out using this. The full size Practice Chart 5055 can be purchased from Admiralty chart agents for a very small sum. All the exercises in the book can be worked out on this.

*Chapter One*

# Introduction to Charts

## Scale

Every boat on passage needs to have on board adequate and up-to-date navigational charts to cover the whole of the proposed journey, including any areas into which she may be diverted. Besides enabling position and course to be plotted, a chart gives information on dangers and also aids to safe pilotage and navigation.

The scale of the chart required depends on how much detail the navigator needs. A small scale chart is adequate for coastal and cross channel planning, but it would not give enough detailed information regarding inshore hazards, anchorages or port entrances. Such information is only found on a larger scale.

The scale, shown under the chart title, gives the number of units, measured on land or sea, which are represented by one unit on the chart; for example, if the scale is 1:200,000 then one inch (or centimetre) on the chart equals 200,000 inches (or centimetres) on land or sea. Practice navigational chart 5055, which is the small scale chart used for examples in this manual, has a scale of 1:150,000.

For a coastal passage the required charts would provide a small scale for the whole passage, a larger scale for congested waters and port approach, and the largest scale available for port and anchorage areas.

## Supply of Charts

Admiralty charts are published by the Hydrographer of the Navy at Taunton and are sold by Admiralty approved Chart Agents. There are also two private firms which publish their own charts, based on information from the Hydrographer: Imray, Laurie, Norie and Wilson Ltd, of St Ives, and Barnacle Marine Ltd, Essex. They both issue catalogues, and their charts are available from most chandlers and nautical booksellers. Foreign countries, of course, also publish their own charts.

ADMIRALTY CHARTS

These coloured navigational charts are designed for use on board all forms of craft and, in areas used predominantly by small boats, emphasis is given to details which will be of use to them.

Coverage is world wide, lists being tabulated in *Catalogue of Admiralty Charts and other Hydrographic Publications*, NP131, with a limited edition, *NP109*, covering the British Isles and North West Europe. Both these catalogues are re-issued annually in January. Other types of charts include:

*Latticed.* Overlaid with position fixing lines for use with various navigational systems such as Decca Navigator, Loran, Omega and Consol.

*Magnetic.* Showing lines of equal magnetic variation and annual change in variation.

*Routeing.* For ocean passage planning, giving details of ocean currents, prevailing winds, routes and distances, and other additional information.

*Ships' Boats.* These are survival charts for emergency use only, printed on waterproof materials, and contained in a plastic wallet along with instructions for their use.

*Instructional.* A low priced copy of selected navigational charts, printed on thinner paper than a normal chart and used for practice plotting by students. They must not be used for navigation as they are uncorrected. 5055 is a practice chart.

*PEXA.* Practice and Exercise Area chart showing areas used by the Ministry of Defence for firing practice and exercise.

IMRAY, LAURIE, NORIE AND WILSON LTD

These are similar in appearance to Admiralty charts. Besides a limited series covering the Caribbean, the principal coverage is of NW Europe.

*Y Charts.* Coloured charts on small format sheets giving large scale coverage of estuaries and rivers, but the series also includes a number of coastal charts on smaller scales. They cover the east and south coasts of England.

*C Charts.* Coloured charts for cuising use and, in most cases, they have inset plans of ports and tidal information. Coverage is most of the British Isles and the North Coast of France. The reverse side of these charts carries a legend of signs and symbols used on the charts.

Both Y and C charts are available plastic laminated.

STANFORDS CHARTS (Published by Barnacle Marine Ltd)

These are coloured charts which fold to a convenient size for easy stowage. Information includes port plans, pilotage notes and tidal diagrams. Coverage is the English Channel, the East Coast from Cromer to Harwich, the Essex Rivers, the Thames Estuary, the English Channel, Poole Harbour and Approaches, the Channel Islands, the N. Brittany coast and the Southern North Sea. Stanfords *ALLWEATHER* charts are printed on waterproof paper.

FOREIGN CHARTS

In some cases it is better to use a chart printed in the country around which the boat is navigating, as a larger scale may be available containing a lot more detail not shown on other charts. The symbols are usually easy to understand. An ideal would be to carry both an English and a foreign chart in such circumstances.

## Chart Correction

For safe navigation, charts must be corrected regularly, in order to incorporate changes in navigational information (buoys, lights, new wrecks or oil rigs etc). This can be done by returning Admiralty charts to a Chart Agent, or by correcting them from the information contained in Admiralty *Notes to Mariners*, Weekly Edition (with an annual summary) or Small Craft Edition. These publications contain notices numbered in sequence throughout the year, listing affected charts, and giving the correction and the number of the previous notice affecting the same charts.

When a chart has been corrected, the number of the notice concerned is inserted in the bottom left-hand margin so that a check can be made that no corrections are missing. Where the correction is difficult to plot by hand a small facsimile stick on portion is provided.

Important changes are promulgated immediately as navigation warnings by Coast Radio Stations. These are collected and issued weekly in *Notices to Mariners*. Temporary changes and details of proposed changes (Preliminary) are suffixed with a (T) or (P) respectively.

If the corrections are extensive, a new edition of the chart is published, announced beforehand in *Notices to Mariners* in the case of Admiralty charts, and all other editions prior to the reprint are cancelled. The date of the new edition is printed in the bottom margin immediately after the date of the original publication.

Admiralty *Notices to Mariners*, Annual Summary, is available free in January, from Mercantile Marine offices, Customs Houses and Chart Agents, and includes information on distress and rescue procedure, warnings by Coast Radio Stations, details of firing practice and exercise areas, and other items of interest to larger shipping. The Weekly Edition, containing mainly chart corrections, is also available free from the same sources.

A Small Craft Edition of *Notices to Mariners*, sold at Chart Agents, is issued four times a year and contains a summary of the corrections to home waters charts and associated publications; use of this saves sorting through the many weekly notices, and is thus much easier for the owner who is correcting his own charts. It also lists the current editions of home waters *Sailing Directions, List of Lights* and *List of Radio Signals* (these publications will be explained later).

Imray charts are corrected from information given in their bulletin, by correction slips issued periodically, or by returning the charts to them. Stanfords charts are corrected by lists of corrections for each chart, which are available free of charge, or by returning the charts to Barnacle Marine Ltd. The date to which these charts are corrected is printed on the chart.

It is important to check on the latest correction of all charts being used, especially those of foreign publication.

## Information on the Chart

*Title and Number.* Before purchasing a chart, it is necessary to know the title and the reference number given to that chart; this information is given in the catalogue. The chart is named according to the area which it covers; for example, practice chart 5055 covers the area between Newhaven and Calais, and its title is *Newhaven to Calais.* The title is placed where it will not interfere with any portion of the chart giving information required for navigation, and the reference number is printed in the top and bottom margins of Admiralty and Imray charts, and in the top margin of Stanfords charts.

*Legend.* This is information printed under the title, such as scale, latitude, measurement units used for depths and heights (metres or fathoms and feet), the type of projection and the authority from which the information was obtained.

*Cautions.* These are warnings of particular hazards, and are either printed near the title or on part of the chart not used for navigation.

*Tidal Streams.* On Admiralty, Imray and Stanfords coastal charts this information is tabulated in columns, referred to high water at the main port, giving the direction and rate of flow of tidal streams at high water and for hours before and after high water. These figures are keyed to a letter on the chart. There may also be tidal diagrams giving the same information.

*Heights and Soundings.* On metric charts, land objects are given in metres above Mean High Water Spring level and depths in metres and decimetres below Chart Datum (Mean High Water Spring level and Chart Datum will be explained later when considering tides). On pre-metric charts, heights are in feet and depths in fathoms and feet. As the datum to which heights and depths are referred may differ from that used for metric charts, the legend of the chart should be carefully studied before use. Most charts for UK waters are now metric.

*Latitude and Longitude Scale.* The latitude scale is along the side margins of the chart, and the longitude scale along the top and bottom margins. The units of measurement used are degrees, minutes and either seconds or tenths of a minute.

*Other Information.* There is, of course, much additional information including hazards, wrecks, obstructions, rocks, buoyage, lights, fog signals, anchorages and a compass rose indicating direction.

## Care of the Chart

Navigational charts are much more expensive than those issued purely for practice instruction, and every care should be taken to prolong their life. Unless subject to a large correction entailing the issue of a new edition, with care they will last for several years; but they must be kept up to date if they are to be useful and safe.

It is best to fold a chart as little as possible as it will wear very quickly along the creases, ideally it should be kept flat in a chart table or folder. Too many charts taken from the folder at one time can cause damage, and lead to confusion in an emergency when information is needed quickly. Charts should be kept dry and not taken into the cockpit; if the navigator has to go on deck, a towel placed along the bottom of the chart will help to absorb some of the water from wet oilskins. There are some ready-made plastic covers available for charts, and some charts are available printed on waterproof or plastic laminated paper. A soft pencil should be used for plotting, and a soft eraser which will not damage the surface of the paper.

## Instruments

Instruments are a matter of personal choice, ranging from a piece of string to every elaborate gadget sold. There is a large choice available, some of which are excellent and some entirely unsuitable for use in an unsteady environment such as the navigating area of a small boat in heavy weather. Many can be costly and not very practical or necessary. Parallel rules are a popular choice, but they tend to be difficult to use on a small chart table. A square protractor is simple and easy to use. The best instruments are the ones with which the navigator is familiar. The following list is a suggested minimum with which to start:-

2B pencils.
Notebook.
Pencil compass.
Dividers (8 inch).
Parallel rule or square protractor.

As well as plotting instruments, when in a practical situation, the navigator will require:-

Steering compass.
Hand bearing compass.
Depth sounder.
Speed or distance indicator.

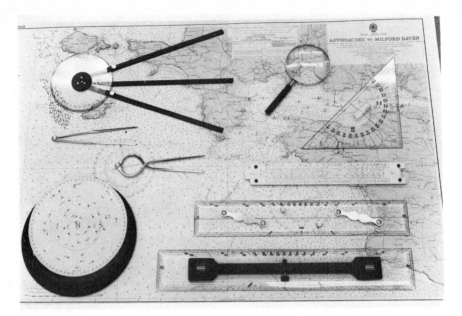

**Plate 1** Sestrel chartroom instruments from Henry Browne & Son Ltd. Left (from top): Station Pointer, plain dividers, single hand dividers, Star Finder. Right (from top): chart magnifier, navigation set square, slide rule, bar type parallel rules, roller type parallel rules.

Reliable clock or watch.
Adequate charts and nautical publications.

## Nautical Publications

A number of publications for use with charts are available from the Hydrographer and from private firms.

### HYDROGRAPHIC PUBLICATIONS

*Symbols and Abbreviations 5011.* This chart in booklet form contains symbols and abbreviations printed on Admiralty charts. It is set out in sections for easy reference and updated by re-issue.

*Tidal Stream Atlas.* See Fig 1. This gives a pictorial representation of tidal streams at hourly intervals referred to high water at the standard port. Direction is indicated by arrows, rate of flow is tabulated in figures and is given for spring and neap tides. For example 22, 47 means a neap rate of 2·2 knots and a spring rate of 4·7 knots (note the absence of a decimal point and the implication of the comma). The port of reference is shown on the cover and on the high water page.

*Admiralty Tide Tables.* Three volumes cover the world. *Volume 1* is for European waters, and the information contained includes times and heights of high and low water for standard ports, tables of secondary differences, tidal curves with special ones for areas where there is a tidal anomaly, heights above chart datum for various ports, and instructions for use together with worked examples.

*Admiralty List of Radio Signals.* There are six volumes, the main ones of interest to small boat users are Volume 2 *Radio Navigational Aids NP282* and Volume 3 *Radio Weather Services NP283.* Corrected by reference to Admiralty *Notices to Mariners,* Weekly Edition.

*Admiralty List of Lights and Fog Signals.* Twelve volumes give world coverage. *Volume A, NP74* covers the British Isles and north coasts of France giving details of lights and fog signals. Corrected by reference to Admiralty *Notices to Mariners,* Weekly Edition.

*Sailing Directions (Pilots) NP1-72.* These give details of land features, off-lying dangers, tidal streams and currents, buoyage systems and information about port entrances and channels. Correction is by revision at intervals of 12 to 15 years, by supplements issued periodically and, for important amendments, by Admiralty *Notices to Mariners.*

COMMERCIAL PUBLICATIONS

Various private firms publish almanacs giving times of tides, tidal stream atlases, radio services, and lists of lights. They also publish sailing directions with similar information to the Admiralty *Sailing Directions;* useful to small boat owners are *Reed's Nautical Almanac, Macmillan and Silk Cut Almanac, Channel West and Solent Almanac* and the *Cruising Association Handbook.*

There is also a wide variety of pilotage books published by private firms, giving extra information to small boat users visiting the area covered. Books such as *North Sea Harbours and Pilotage, Normandy Harbours and Pilotage, North Brittany Pilot, North Biscay Pilot* and *South Biscay Pilot* (all published by Adlard Coles Ltd) are the result of private survey by the authors concerned, and should always be used in conjunction with up-to-date navigational charts. They are, however, written from the yachtsman's point of view, and have a long and fine reputation for usability and value for money. They seem expensive to buy at the time but they can save their value many times over in use.

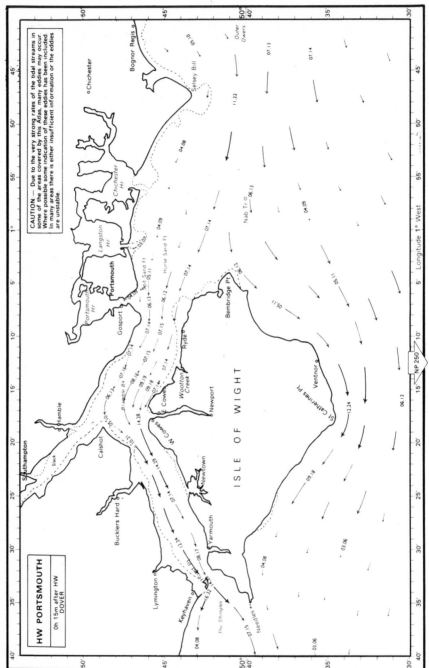

**Fig 1** A page from NP337, the Tidal Stream Atlas for Solent and Adjacent Waters. Produced with the sanction of the Controller HM Stationery Office and of the Hydrographer of the Navy.

# QUESTION PAPER 1 – INTRODUCTION TO CHARTS

Answers on page 179

1.1 What is the scale of practice chart 5055?

1.2 If you were asked to purchase charts and publications for a coastal passage, what would be your choice?

1.3 In what publications would you find a list of Admiralty chart agents?

1.4 What are *cautions* as referred to on a chart?

1.5 If you were in doubt regarding one of the symbols on an Admiralty chart, which publication would you consult?

1.6 What information is contained in *Sailing Directions*?

1.7 How are the following charts corrected;
  (a) Stanford.
  (b) Imray.
  (c) Admiralty.

1.8 In what publications would you look to find;
  (a) The area covered by a particular chart.
  (b) The title of the chart.
  (c) The number of the chart.

1.9 What are the advantages and disadvantages of Admiralty *Notices to Mariners* Small Craft Edition?

1.10 What units of measurement are used for depths and heights on a metric chart?

## Chapter Two

# What is a Chart?

For navigational purposes, it is necessary to have a flat diagram of the earth's surface, with co-ordinates to enable a position to be identified. Such a diagram, called a map or chart, presents the cartographer with a problem because the earth cannot be cut down the middle and laid out flat. This is resolved by projecting an image of the earth's spherical form on to a flat surface by one of several methods. Before projection, the surface of the earth is overlaid with imaginary horizontal and vertical lines, used as reference points, which form circles and half circles on its surface; any circle whose plane passes through the centre of the earth is called a Great Circle, and its circumference represents the shortest distance between any two points along it. The network formed by these horizontal and vertical lines is called the graticule of the chart.

## Parallels of Latitude

The great circle whose plane passes horizontally through the centre of the earth, is called the Equator, and it divides the earth into the northern and southern hemispheres; Fig 2.1. Parallel to the equator at intervals both north and south are small circles (the planes of which do not pass through the centre of the earth), called Parallels of Latitude. These are graduated at one degree intervals, from zero degrees at the equator to ninety degrees at the North and South Poles. The North and South Poles mark the extremities of the earth's axis.

These one degree intervals are subdivided into sixty divisions called minutes, and then further divided either into tenths of a minute or into sixty parts called seconds; therefore, $60'' = 1'$; $60' = 1°$; $90° = 1$ right angle.

Sign for seconds is "
Sign for minutes is '
Sign for degrees is °

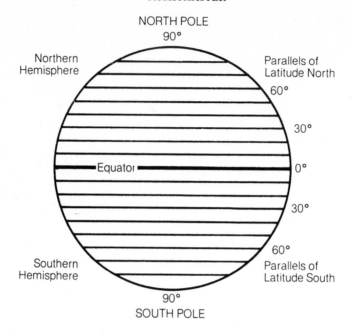

**Fig 2.1** Parallels of latitude are parallel to the equator, and range from 0° to 90° north and south.

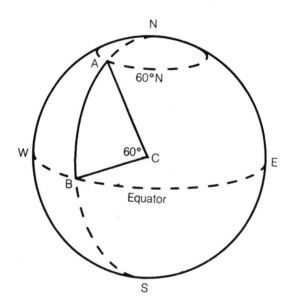

**Fig 2.2** Latitude north or south is determined by the angle subtended at the centre of the earth between it and the equator. Here, for example, 60°N is shown as subtending an angle of 60° at the centre of the earth.

*Latitude* is the angular measurement subtended at the centre of the earth between the equator and the parallel of latitude of the observer, annotated as being either North or South of the equator, see Fig 2.2.

EXAMPLE 1

Fifty degrees, ten point five minutes would be written 50° 10'·5 (the minute sign is placed before the decimal point). Fifty degrees, ten minutes, thirty seconds would be written 50° 10' 30". Note that these two values are exactly the same, because thirty seconds of latitude is half a minute. It is also necessary to indicate whether the latitude is in the northern or southern hemisphere by placing N or S after the figures: 50° 10'·5N.

## Meridians of Longitude

The vertical lines which form half great circles between the North and South Poles are called Meridians of Longitude. The meridian which passes through Greenwich Observatory in London is called the Greenwich meridian and it is the datum line for the other meridians which are spaced east and west from it, Fig 2.3. These vertical divisions start at zero degrees at Greenwhich meridian and continue to one hundred and eighty degrees either east or west of Greenwich. The one hundred and eightieth meridian is a continuation of the Greenwich meridian, and together they form a great circle dividing the earth into the eastern and western hemispheres.

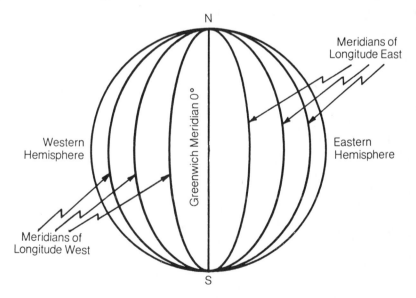

**Fig 2.3** Meridians of longitude run from pole to pole, over the earth's surface. The Meridian passing through Greenwich is taken as 0°, and is called the Greenwich Meridian. Longitude is either east or west of this datum line, from 0° to 180°.

The meridians are graduated in the same manner as the latitude scale into degrees, minutes, and either tenths of a minute or seconds.

*Longitude* is the angle subtended at the axis of the earth between Greenwich meridian and the meridian of the observer, Fig 2.4.

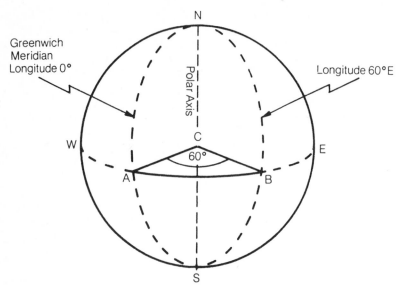

**Fig 2.4** Longitude east or west is determined by the angle subtended at the earth's axis between it and the Greenwich Meridian. Here, point B is shown to lie at longitude 60°E.

EXAMPLE 2

Four degrees, six point four minutes would be written, 4° 6'·4. Four degrees, six minutes, thirty seconds would be written, 4° 6' 30". To indicate whether the longitude is east or west of Greenwich an E or W is placed after the figures: 4° 6'·4W.

## The Mercator Projection

This type of chart was used as long ago as the sixteenth century. It is constructed by projecting imaginary lines from the centre of the earth through the surface of the earth on to a cylinder which is then opened out. For the convenience of the cartographer it has been slightly distorted from a true radial projection to produce a chart with the following properties:

1. The equator appears as a straight line.
2. Parallels of latitude are straight lines equidistant from the equator.

3. Meridians of longitude are straight lines crossing the parallels at right angles.
4. A straight line, such as a track, drawn from one position to another crosses each meridian at the same angle.

Because meridians are projected as straight lines, distortion occurs towards the poles as the sphere is 'opened' out and, if no compensation were made, land masses would only appear normal at the equator, elsewhere they would appear to have increased in width but not in height. To counteract this, the parallels are moved a corresponding distance apart, which makes the land masses the correct proportional shape, but increases their area, and so in higher latitudes a small island would appear to be much larger than an island of the same size at a lower latitude if represented on the same chart. As the poles are approached the distortion becomes extreme and this type of projection cannot be employed.

The mercator projection chart is constructed by using a constant unit called a meridional part, which is equal to one minute of longitude along the equator. To determine where to draw a parallel of latitude either north or south of the equator, the number of meridional parts between the equator and the desired latitude is found either by calculation or by reference to a special table tabulated in some nautical almanacs:

EXAMPLE 3

| Latitude | Meridional Parts |
|----------|------------------|
| 7° | 418·20 |
| 14° | 842·83 |

If the meridional parts remain the same, doubling the degrees from 7 to 14 would produce 836·4. But 842·83 is an increase of 6·43 on that figure, showing that the length of a minute of arc on the latitude scale increases as latitude increases. The longitude scale is constant, therefore one minute of arc on this scale will only equal one minute of arc on the latitude scale *at the equator*. For this reason, measurement of distance on the chart is made along the latitude scale *always level with the area of interest*; never along the longitude scale, which is used only as a co-ordinate to find a position.

One minute of arc along the latitude scale is called a nautical mile. Because it varies slightly in length with latitude, a mean value of 6076 feet is used for most navigational purposes. It is divided into tenths, each tenth, for convenience of measurement, is 600 feet (the exact metric distance of a nautical mile has been standardised internationally at 1852 metres).

A measurement of one nautical mile per hour, called a knot, refers to speed at sea.

GREAT CIRCLE

The shortest distance between two points on a mercator chart is a great circle which, when plotted, would appear as a curve. Because the great circle track does not cross all meridians at the same angle on this type of projection, the course would have to be constantly altered for the track to be maintained. The long distance navigator draws a great circle track and then divides it into a series of straight lines called rhumb lines.

RHUMB LINE

A rhumb line crosses all meridians at the same angle and appears on a mercator chart as a straight line; on a sphere it would appear as a curve.

Although a rhumb line is not the shortest distance between two points, over a small distance (up to 600 miles) the difference is negligible, and the convenience of maintaining one course and being able to draw a straight line on the chart is considerable, so it is used for short passages.

## Gnomonic Projection

A gnomonic projection is the projection of the earth's surface onto a tangent plane (a plane touching the earth's surface at one point); normally, for convenience, this point is the north or south pole. The meridians of longitude and parallels of latitude appear as curves, except in a Polar Gnomonic Projection where the meridians are straight lines radiating from the poles. A great circle track appears as a straight line so, given the co-ordinates of two places on the earth, a straight line can be drawn between them. The points at which this line crosses various meridians and parallels can be determined, and transferred to an appropriate mercator chart as a series of rhumb lines. Thus the courses to steer to achieve a near great circle track can be determined.

# QUESTION PAPER 2 – WHAT IS A CHART?

Answers on page 180

2.1   What is a great circle?

2.2   What is a rhumb line?

2.3   Why is it necessary to measure distance only along the latitude scale level with (or opposite to) your track?

2.4   Express in figures:
(a)  Thirty degrees, two point one minutes north.
(b)  Two degrees, six point eight minutes west.

2.5   Why is it not possible to construct a mercator projection chart for areas near the south pole?

*Chapter Three*

# Position and Direction

The co-ordinates on the latitude and longitude scales are used to find a position on the chart. On chart 5055 the scales are graduated in degrees, minutes and decimal points of a minute. Along the top and bottom scale (about the middle of the chart), is the figure 1°, next to which at the bottom of the chart is written 'East from Greenwich'; this means that the area shown on the chart is east of the Greenwich meridian and so the numbers which occur at 5 minute intervals along this scale will increase from 5' to 55' towards the right hand side of the chart. If the area had been west of Greenwich, the figures would have increased towards the left hand side of the chart. There is a line drawn from the top to the bottom of the chart at 1° and also at every 20 minute interval along the longitude scale. These reference lines (meridians) make measurement easier.

On the latitude scale to the left and right is the large figure 51°, indicating that this point is 51° north of the equator. Reference lines (parallels) are drawn across the chart at 51° and at 15 minute intervals either side of 51°. The numbers indicating minutes always increase from the equator towards the poles between degrees.

## Position

The next step is to use plotting instruments to find a position on chart 5055. For the examples a parallel rule and dividers are used, but the principle is the same with other types of plotting instruments.

The position, expressed as latitude and longitude, of the lightvessel on the Varne Bank is required:

First the latitude is found by placing the edge of the rule along the nearest parallel which is 51°. The rule is kept horizontal to this parallel and opened out slightly to intersect the small circle at the bottom of the lightvessel. The rule will also intersect the latitude scale on the right hand side of the chart indicating 51° 1'·3N. Now the dividers are similarly used to measure the longitude from the nearest meridian which is 1° 20'·0E. The longitude is 1° 24'·0E. It is customary to express latitude first and then longitude.

To find a position when given the co-ordinates, the procedure is reversed. It is possible to measure latitude and longitude on the chart using only a parallel rule or dividers, but it is quicker and more convenient to use both.

## Direction

The compass rose is the reference on a chart for direction. It has an outer circle which is graduated in degrees from 0 to 359, with 0 in the direction of true north. The inner ring is similarly graduated, but 0 is in the direction of magnetic north (for discussion of magnetic north see chapter 4).

Direction is normally indicated using a three figure notation, for example: 003°, 030°, 148°.

### EXAMPLE 4

To find the direction from the Varne Lightvessel in Fig 3.1 to the western entrance to Dover Harbour, the parallel rule is placed so that it cuts through both places and then 'walked' across the chart by opening and closing until the edge passes through the dot in the centre of the compass rose. The rule will cut the edge of the rose at two places: 155° and 335° but, as the required direction is from right to left, 335° is the correct answer. The letter T is placed after the figures to indicate that it is a true direction which means that no allowance has yet been made for magnetic influences, ie 335°T. When a known direction is to be plotted, the rule is first placed across the compass rose with the edge passing through the dot in the middle of the rose and cutting the required figure, and is then 'walked' across the chart to the desired position.

When using graduated plotting instruments such as a graduated parallel rule or a square protractor, it is unnecessary to use the compass rose, the nearest meridian will suffice.

## Bearing

A bearing is the direction of one object taken from another, an example is shown in Fig 3.2. In this example, church A bears 180° from the boat; the boat bears 000° from church A, lighthouse B bears 315° from the boat; the boat bears 135° from lighthouse B.

An alternative to a true bearing is a bearing relative to the boat's heading (called a relative bearing). This is measured in degrees to the right (starboard) or the left (port) of the boat's heading and is sometimes indicated by the prefix *green* for starboard or *red* for port, thus an object on the starboard beam would be on a bearing of green 90°, and one on the port bow would be red 45°. For relative bearings the full three figure notation is not used.

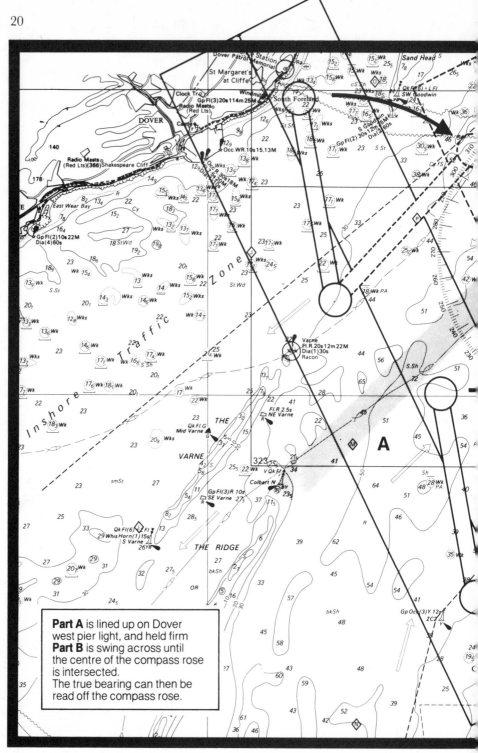

**Fig 3.1** The use of parallel rules demonstrated. The 'fixed' edge of the rule is lined up on the course line, and then the other edge moved to the nearest compass rose, which is conveniently close here. Where it is further away, the rules have to be 'walked' across the chart, which must be done carefully to avoid slipping.

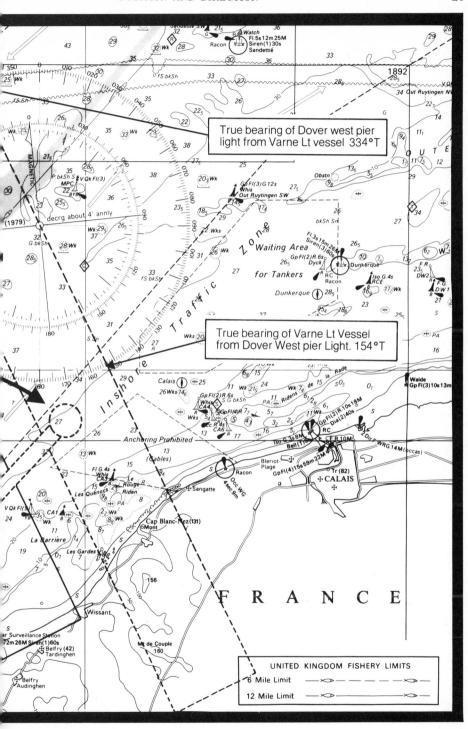

True bearing of Dover west pier light from Varne Lt vessel 334°T

True bearing of Varne Lt Vessel from Dover West pier Light. 154°T

FRANCE

| UNITED KINGDOM FISHERY LIMITS | | |
| --- | --- | --- |
| 6 Mile Limit | | |
| 12 Mile Limit | | |

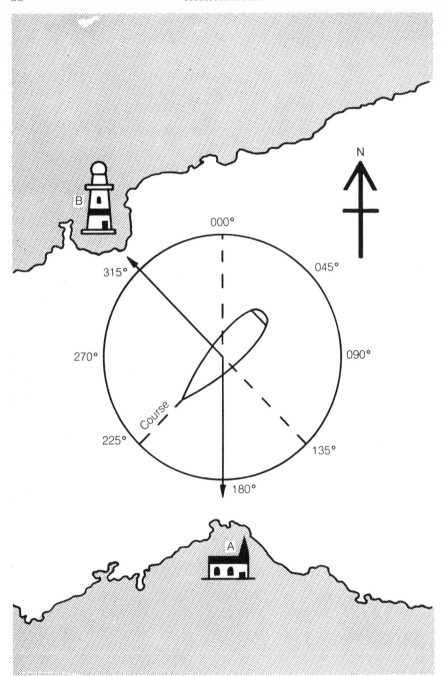

**Fig 3.2** Bearings are always described as from the point of sighting to the object being sighted. Here the church A bears 180°T from the vessel, and the lighthouse B bears 315° T from the vessel. The bearings of the vessel from A and B are the reciprocals of these.

In the example shown in Fig 3.3 the boat's heading is 090°, the relative bearings red 45° and green 90° become true bearings of 045° and 180° respectively.

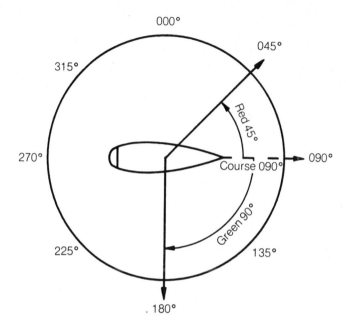

**Fig 3.3** Relative bearings. An object sighted bearing 045° from a vessel on a heading of 090° could be equally said to bear Red 45°; and an object bearing 180° thus bears Green 90°.

# QUESTION PAPER 3 – POSITION AND DIRECTION

Answers on page 180

3.1   What is the bearing in three figure notation of a relative bearing of red 45° if the boat's heading is 085°T?

3.2   What is the position of:
(a)  Varne Light Vessel.
(b)  South cardinal buoy on SW end of The Varne.
(c)  West cardinal buoy about 3½ miles west of Cap Blanc-Nez.

3.3   What is the bearing of the lighthouse at Folkestone from Varne Light Vessel?

3.4   What is the track from one mile south of Dungeness lighthouse, Qk Fl.R, to Varne Light Vessel?

3.5   What is the chart symbol in position 50° 53'·0N, 1° 0'·6E?

*Chapter Four*

# The Magnetic Compass

### The Steering Compass

This is an instrument used to help the helmsman steer a course. It consists of a bowl, part of which is transparent, filled with liquid and containing a graduated card mounted on a pivot. The graduations on the compass card may vary; on some of the older types it may be divided into 32 points, each point being separated by a sector of 11¼°. The points are named according to the nearest cardinal mark (N E S W) or half cardinal mark

**Plate 2** Sestrel bulkhead bracket mounting compass from Henry Browne & Son Ltd, for tiller-steered yachts and small commercial craft.

**Plate 3** Sestrel porthole compass from Henry Browne & Son Ltd.

(NE SE SW NW), for example the north to east quadrant would be: N, N by E, NNE, NE by N, NE, NE by E, ENE, E by N, E (the wind direction is given in the shipping forecast using this system). Most compasses are now graduated in degrees, or degrees and cardinal and half cardinal marks. For the sake of clarity the last figure is often omitted on the card from the degrees; 60 would be shown as 6 and 150 as 15. The spacing of the markings may be every 5 or 10 degrees, or less on a larger compass card. (It is not practical to steer a course between the markings on the compass card and so the navigator should allow for this.)

Attached to the compass card are magnets which provide the north seeking force to the compass card.

There is a line marked on the fixed part of the compass called a lubber line, which must lie in the fore and aft line of the boat when the compass is installed.

The north point of the compass card, because of the location of the magnets, will point to magnetic north, providing there are no other magnetic influences (see *Variation* below). The course the boat is sailing is indicated by the reading on the compass card scale lined up with the lubber line. If the helmsman is not positioned directly behind the centre of

**Fig 4.1** Two examples of a compass card. The zero is left off the figures for convenience; thus for example 34 is 340°, and 4 is 040°.

the compass, the wrong figure will be read as parallax will occur. When the course is altered, the boat swings around the compass card; the card itself does not move.

Before the course plotted on the chart (true course) can be steered by the helmsman, an allowance has to be made for magnetic influences affecting the compass.

The directional properties of the compass are controlled partly by the earth's magnetic field, partly by close proximity of magnetic objects which attract or repel the magnets contained within the card and, especially in a steel hulled boat, partly by any permanent magnetic field developed during construction.

## Variation

This is the effect upon the compass caused by the earth's magnetic field.

The earth has certain magnetic properties which centre around the True north pole and the True south pole. Like a magnet it has a force field composed of lines of force called magnetic meridians, which terminate at the north and south magnetic poles; fig 4.2. Unlike true meridians which form half great circles between the true poles, magnetic meridians do not follow a regular pattern, nor are the north and south magnetic poles directly opposite each other.

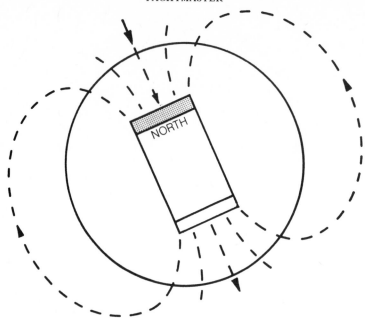

**Fig 4.2** The magnetic field of the earth shown in diagrammatic form; the lines of force flow from north to south in the earth's core, but from south to north on the surface. This is why the compass needle points north.

The position of these poles changes slightly each year as they describe a small circle around the true poles.

The magnet on the compass card takes up a position in line with the nearest magnetic meridian, pointing to magnetic north (assuming that there is no other direction influence acting upon it). The angle between the magnetic meridian in which the compass magnet lies and the true meridian, which is the one shown on the chart, is magnetic variation. If the deflection is to the right of true north variation is called east, and if the deflection is to the left of true north variation is called west. When converting a true course to a magnetic course, westerly variation is added, easterly variation subtracted. When converting a magnetic course to a true course, westerly variation is subtracted, easterly variation added.

Whether a course is true or magnetic is indicated by placing a letter T or a letter M after the degrees:

105°T          111°M

(in this case the variation is 6°W).

HOW TO FIND VARIATION

Refer to the compass rose on chart 5055 between Dover and Calais; there is an inner and outer ring both graduated for 360°. The outer ring applies to

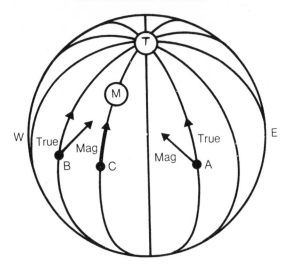

**Fig 4.3** Variation. Magnetic north M is offset slightly from true north T, so the variation between the two will depend on where you are on the earth's surface in relation to them. At point B variation is East, at A it is West, whilst at C the variation is nil since true and magnetic north are directly in line.

true north with no allowance for variation, but on the inner ring the variation has been applied. Because the position of magnetic north changes every year, the information given on this inner ring is only valid for the year the chart was printed, and for this reason the outer ring is usually used, applying the required correction for the year in question. Above the line which is across the middle of the rose is noted the amount of variation to be applied, the year, whether variation is east or west and the rate of annual change. This particular compass rose states:

Variation 5° 45′W (1979) decreasing about 4′ annually

If the course steered were 100°T and the year 1981, the variation would have decreased 8′ making the variation for 1981 5° 37′W and so the magnetic course would be 106° to the nearest degree (remember to place the letter M after a magnetic course, 106°M, to show that variation has been applied).

The nearest compass rose to the boat's position should be used as variation changes according to geographical position. (Look at the variation on the other compass rose on chart 5055).

It is difficult to calculate very far ahead the exact amount of variation applicable to every part of the earth, because the position of the magnetic poles and meridians is constantly changing. The amount of this change cannot be accurately estimated except over a short period and so, if a chart has not been re-issued for a long time, the information on the compass rose may be incorrect. A special magnetic chart is produced by the Hydrographic Office, overlaid with lines joining places where the variation is equal and showing the annual change. This chart is re-issued regularly and the information on it is more likely to be accurate than an out of date compass rose. However, it will be seen on chart 5055 that the annual change is very small, so that it takes over ten years to alter one degree, and so two or three years can usually be ignored.

## Deviation

Deviation is the effect upon the compass magnet of the boat's magnetic field caused by the close proximity of ferrous metal, DC electrical equipment or electronic equipment containing magnets. It can also be caused by the permanent magnetic field induced in the hard iron parts of the boat during construction (this applies basically to a steel boat).

The earth's magnetic field induces a temporary local magnetic field in the soft iron parts of the boat and her fittings. This field varies depending on the direction of the boat's heading; a deviation table can be made by measuring the deviation for different headings.

Because the compass is affected by magnetic objects within the boat, it should be sited well away from the engine and any equipment likely to cause trouble. Any DC equipment when switched on will create a magnetic field which can be reduced by twisting together the positive and negative supply leads.

Deviation can cause the compass magnets to be deflected either east or west, but the correction is applied in the same way as that for variation. When converting a magnetic course to a compass course, westerly deviation is added, easterly deviation subtracted. When converting a compass course to a magnetic course, westerly deviation is subtracted, easterly deviation added.

A letter C placed after the degrees indicates a compass course, which means that both variation and deviation have been applied to a true course to give a course to steer.

When variation and deviation are combined the resultant sum is called compass error (CE).

EXAMPLE 5

| Course | 260°T | 260°T |
|---|---|---|
| Variation | 5°W | |
| | 265°M  or CE | 2°E (+5°W −7°E) |
| Deviation | 7°E | |
| | 258°C | 258°C |

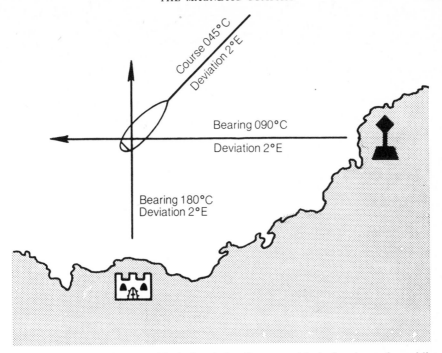

**Fig 4.4** Deviation changes with the boat's heading, not with the bearings taken whilst on that heading. Thus if the deviation on heading 045° is 2°E, the deviation remains 2°E for bearings taken on objects bearing, for example, 090° and 180°. Note that when bearings are plotted on the chart as position lines, the arrowhead is drawn as from the object to the boat, though the bearing is taken from the boat.

The deviation is always applied with reference to the boat's heading, and any bearings taken with the steering compass whilst on that heading will have the same deviation as the heading; fig 4.4.

EXAMPLE 6

A boat steering a course of 265°T, variation 5°E, deviation 10°W has taken three bearings using the steering compass:

334°C          180°C          030°C

Variation is 5°E, and deviation will be 10°W for *all three bearings*. The true bearings will be:

329°T          175°T          025°T

If the bearings had been taken with a hand bearing compass which was held well away from and not affected by the boat's magnetic influences, the bearings taken (to arrive at the same answers) would have been: 324°M 170°M 020°M (see hand bearing compass below).

## Heeling Error

A change of deviation of the compass may occur when the boat is heeled, due to the magnetic influences being placed in a different position relative to the compass. Compensation for heeling error is a complicated matter and should be done by a qualified compass adjuster.

Generally speaking, on a northerly or southerly course any heeling error if present will be maximum, and on an easterly or westerly course it will be minimum. The error will be constant for the same angle of heel.

## Finding Deviation

Before the compass bearing on a steering compass can be corrected to give a true bearing, the deviation for the compass on several headings needs to be determined to make up a deviation card; fig 4.5. The exercise carried out to gain this information is called swinging the boat for deviation. There are several methods of doing this, three of which are discussed here, together with the advantages and disadvantages of each method:

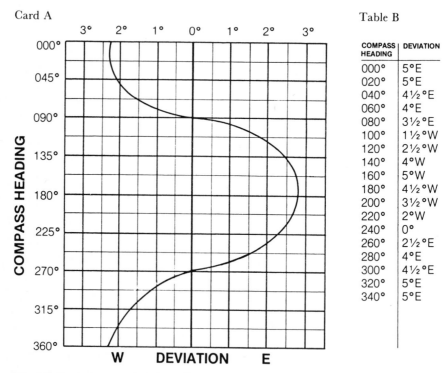

Card A

Table B

| COMPASS HEADING | DEVIATION |
|---|---|
| 000° | 5°E |
| 020° | 5°E |
| 040° | 4½°E |
| 060° | 4°E |
| 080° | 3½°E |
| 100° | 1½°W |
| 120° | 2½°W |
| 140° | 4°W |
| 160° | 5°W |
| 180° | 4½°W |
| 200° | 3½°W |
| 220° | 2°W |
| 240° | 0° |
| 260° | 2½°E |
| 280° | 4°E |
| 300° | 4½°E |
| 320° | 5°E |
| 340° | 5°E |

**Fig 4.5** Deviation on a boat's compass can either be committed to graph form as on the card A, or tabulated at regular intervals as on the Table B. Note that Table A and Card B refer to different compasses, and therefore reveal different deviations on identical headings. The intervals should be chosen so that it is easy to interpolate between them.

USING THE STEERING COMPASS

A suitable transit is found which is shown on the chart. It should be clearly visible but as far away as possible to avoid error.

The boat is steered across this transit on eight or more headings, and the compass bearing of the transit is noted as it is crossed on each heading. The compass bearing on each heading is later compared with the magnetic bearing of the transit which has been converted from the true bearing by the application of variation. Any difference found between the two figures is the deviation for that particular heading only.

*Advantages*
1. Only two people are required, one to keep the boat on course and one to note the compass readings.
2. Less preparation.

*Disadvantages*
1. In a sailing boat there will be one course directly into the wind, where no check of deviation can be made.
2. The boat will be on the transit for a fraction of a second only and it needs a steady helmsman to keep the boat on course.
3. Many small boats do not have the steering compass in a position where there is an all round view of the horizon.

USING THE HAND BEARING COMPASS

The boat is anchored by the bows and stern. A boat hook or other suitable object is positioned vertically in the centre line of the boat to act as a transit with the mast when the boat is viewed from astern. Two people stay on the boat, one to watch the compass reading and one to relay signals. Two people with a hand bearing compass are in the dinghy, one rowing and one taking the bearings.

The dinghy is rowed directly astern of the boat completely clear of any magnetic influences from the boat, and held in this position while the transit of the mast and the boat hook is lined up. The bearing obtained from the hand bearing compass on the transit is later compared with the reading of the steering compass for that heading, the difference being the deviation. The stern anchor is then moved to position the boat on a new heading (45° round). This is done on eight equidistant headings.

*Advantages*
1. An all round view from the steering compass is unnecessary.
2. Land transits are not required, so there is more time to take each bearing.
3. The boat can be heeled to find out if it affects the compass.
4. No adjustment for variation has to be made to bearings, as a compass bearing is being compared with a magnetic bearing.

*Disadvantages*
1. More people needed.
2. More preparation.
3. Difficult in areas where there is a tidal stream or when there is a strong wind.
4. Time consuming as the anchor has to be raised and lowered each time.

USING A DISTANT CONSPICUOUS LANDMARK

The boat is anchored. The dinghy is used to tow the stern of the boat round in a circle. From the steering compass using an azimuth ring, a bearing is taken of a conspicuous landmark which is a considerable distance away. This is done on headings at 45° intervals. The bearing obtained is compared with the magnetic bearing to produce a deviation table. The magnetic bearing can be deduced either by measuring the true bearing from the chart and applying variation or by a direct reading from the hand bearing compass.

*Advantages*
1. Quick with relatively little preparation.

*Disadvantages*
2. Calm conditions required.

The method used will depend upon the type of boat, type of compass and where it is sited, and the number of people available. All methods require:

1. An additional table to be made with the engine running.
2. All gear likely to influence the compass stowed in its normal seagoing position.
3. At least eight equidistant headings to be taken.

The deviations obtained are only valid as long as the compass is used in the position in which it was sited when the swing for deviation was done. Should the compass be moved and used in another position, the swing must be done again. It should be done regularly every season.

If the deviation is found to be more than 3 or 4 degrees on any heading, the assistance of a compass adjuster is required, who will position pieces of soft iron or small magnets around the compass to eliminate most of the errors. This is a complicated procedure and should not be attempted by the unskilled.

As it is impossible to eliminate every small error, after the compass has been adjusted the boat should again be swung for deviation and a deviation card made up.

## Siting a Compass

It is not often possible to achieve the ideal position to site the steering compass, especially in a small boat, but the following points should be considered when choosing this site:

1. Either on the centre line of the boat with the fore and aft line on the compass lined up with the fore and aft line of the boat, or to one side of the boat with the fore and aft line on the compass lined up parallel to the fore and aft line of the boat.
2. Well away from ferrous metals, magnetic and electronic equipment; at least one metre from large objects such as the engine or any stowed anchors.
3. Where it will not get damaged in rough weather by the helmsman or crew using it as a grab handle or stepping on it, or by loose objects on the boat.
4. Where the helmsman can best see it clearly from the steering position without parallax.
5. With an all round view of the horizon (this is rarely possible) so that if fitted with an azimuth ring, it can be used for taking bearings as well as for steering.
6. Firmly secured.

## Hand Bearing Compass

This is a compass used for taking bearings, and if held well away from magnetic materials will have negligible deviation. It is difficult, however, on a small boat to move away from all such influences. It is not possible to make up a deviation card for a hand bearing compass because it will not be used in exactly the same place every time.

It is subject to variation in exactly the same way as the steering compass and this is the only correction which should be applied to it.

## Azimuth Ring

A compass which is sited with an all round view of the horizon needs a proper sighting mechanism if an accurate bearing is to be taken. A prism sight is mounted on an azimuth ring, which rotates around the outside edge of the compass bowl, so that it can be lined up on a target and the bearing read. This is also sometimes called a ring sight or an azimuth mirror. (Fig 4.6)

## Pelorus

When the steering compass is sited so that it does not command an all

**Plate 4** Sestrel Radiant prismatic handbearing compass from Henry Browne & Son Ltd.

**Fig 4.6** An azimuth ring or mirror.          **Fig 4.7** A pelorus.

round view of the horizon, bearings relative to the boat's head or to the compass course can be taken by means of a pelorus. (Fig 4.7)

This is a flat disc graduated to 360°, mounted on a base with a pivot so that the disc rotates. The base has a lubber line which is lined up in the fore and aft line of the boat when the pelorus is installed, there is also a sight which pivots independent of the disc. The pelorus should be fixed to the boat in a position where there is an all round view of the horizon and where it will suffer no damage.

To take a bearing the course being steered is found on the disc which is then moved round so that this course is in line with the lubber line. The pelorus has now become a repeater of the steering compass. The object chosen is lined up in the sight and the bearing noted. Alternatively the zero or north point of the pelorus can be lined up fore and aft so that the bearings become relative to the boat's head.

# QUESTION PAPER 4 – THE MAGNETIC COMPASS

Answers on page 180

4.1   What is a lubber line?

4.2   Where would you find variation for a particular area?

4.3   What considerations influence the siting of a steering compass?

4.4   Using variation from chart 5055 (the compass rose between Dover and Calais), for the year of the chart, convert the following courses to true (to the nearest degree):
   (a) 034°M
   (b) 298°M
   (c) 136°M

4.5   Using variation from chart 5055 (the compass rose between Dover and Calais), for the year of the chart, and the deviation table B (Fig 4.5), with a boat's course of 315°C, what are the true bearings for the following:
   (a) 115°C
   (b) 151°C
   (c) 219°C

4.6   Why is it not practical to make up a deviation card for the hand bearing compass?

4.7   Using deviation card A in Fig 4.5, what are the magnetic courses to the nearest degree for the following:
   (a) 045°C
   (b) 214°C
   (c) 315°C

## Chapter Five

# What is the Position?

During a passage, it is important that the navigator knows where the boat is at all times. Sometimes two or more position lines may be used to provide a *fix*, which is a most accurate method as no allowance has to be made for any sideways deflection caused by the wind (leeway), or for tidal influences. See Chapter 7.

### Dead Reckoning Position (DR)

It is not always possible to fix the boat's position at frequent regular intervals, because suitable objects from which to take bearings may not be available. It is necessary, therefore, to keep a record of courses steered and distances travelled to enable an approximate position to be maintained; this will not be as accurate as a fix.

The position arrived at by this method, when only course steered and distance travelled are taken into account, is called a Dead Reckoning Position (DR), and it is shown on the chart by a cross alongside which is written the time and the log reading in brackets.

### Estimated Position (EP)

When the deflection caused by the wind (leeway), and the effects of the tidal stream are applied to the DR position, the position obtained is called an Estimated Position (EP), shown on the chart by a triangle with a dot in the centre, alongside which is written the time and the log reading in brackets. An estimated position is more accurate that a dead reckoning position but not as good as a fix.

EXAMPLE 7

If at 1200 a boat were in a position 1 mile south of Dungeness New Lighthouse (shown on chart 5055), maintaining a speed of 5 knots and steering a course directly towards the S Goodwin Light Vessel, west of

Dover, she would arrive 4 hours 42 minutes later (at 1642), provided that her speed and course remained constant and there were no wind and no tidal stream. S Goodwin Light Vessel would be her DR position.

If there were a north wind blowing the boat sideways, this leeway would cause her to be south of this DR position, provided there were still no tidal stream; her distance run over the ground would be the same. If there were also a tidal stream pushing her to the south her estimated position would be even further away from the DR; her EP will only be completely accurate if the calculations for leeway and tidal stream are correct.

## Effect of The Wind (Leeway)

The angle of leeway differs with the course of the boat relative to the wind; if the boat is sailing as close to the wind as possible (close hauled) the leeway is maximum, and if the wind is astern (running) it is nil. Different types of boat will not be affected in the same way, even in identical conditions; much depends on the depth of the keel and on the whole underwater profile. The speed at which the boat is travelling and the strength of the wind also affect leeway, which will be maximum at slow speeds in strong winds. A rough estimate of how much leeway a boat is making can be found by taking the difference between the reciprocal of the boat's course and a bearing taken of the wake to give the leeway angle in degrees; fig 5.1.

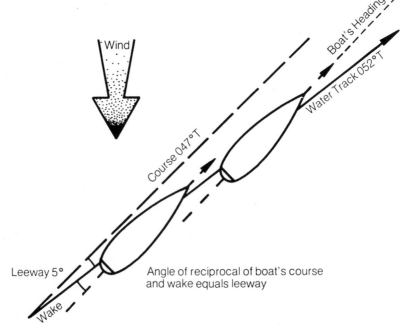

**Fig 5.1** The water track is the result of leeway being applied to the course steered. Leeway can be estimated fairly accurately by looking at the boat's wake in relation to the course being steered.

Leeway always has to be applied away from the direction the wind is blowing when plotting an estimated position, because the boat will have been blown sideways downwind.

EXAMPLE 8

A boat is steering a course of 047°T, there is a northerly wind causing 5° leeway:

Course 047°T + 5° leeway (applied downwind) = 052°T

Although the boat is heading in the direction of 047°T, she is travelling along a track of 052°T. This track, called *water track*, is the one which is plotted on the chart, *not* the course of 047°T; fig 5.1

## Effects Of The Tidal Stream

If the tidal stream is from ahead or astern, only the boat's speed over the ground will be affected. If the tidal stream is acting across the course of the boat she will be set sideways at a rate dependent on the set (direction) and rate (speed) of the stream; fig 5.2. When plotting an estimated position (EP), the set and drift (the distance covered in a given time) is found from the tidal stream data given on the chart, and is applied to the end of the water track. The drift is determined by the rate of the stream and the time the boat has been travelling. For example, if the boat had travelled 4 nautical miles in one hour and the tidal stream was at a rate of 1 knot (1 nautical mile per hour), then a distance corresponding to 1 hour of tidal stream (1 mile measured as 1 minute on the latitude scale) would be applied to the end of the line representing the water track. The tidal stream inset on chart 5055 tabulates hourly the direction towards which the tidal stream flows and its rate in knots. It is convenient to plot on the chart intervals of one hour, but often this is not possible. When the distance plotted is for a period of more or less than one hour, the amount of tidal stream applied must be for the same period. This means that if the boat had been travelling for half an hour, then half the amount of the rate tabulated in the tidal stream inset on the chart would be used.

EXAMPLE 9

A boat has steered a course of 095°T for a period of one hour from position A in fig 5.3. The boat's speed was 4 knots and the tidal stream was 170°T 1 knot; there was 10° leeway due to a northerly wind.

1. Apply the leeway downwind, giving a water track of 105°T. This track is drawn on the chart.
2. Measure a distance of 4 miles (from the latitude scale), and mark the

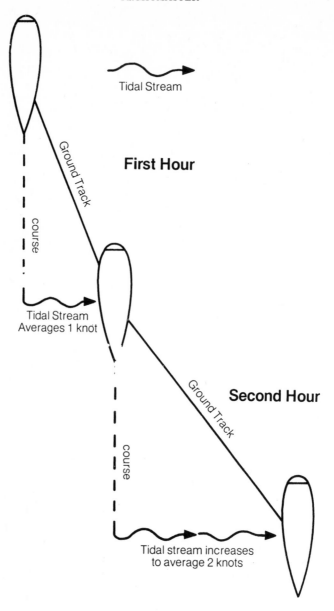

**Fig 5.2** The effect of tidal stream. Here the actual ground track of the boat is significantly affected, despite the constant course steered by the helmsman.

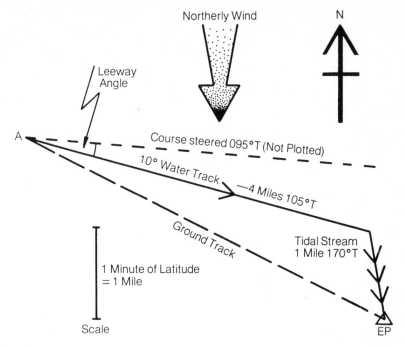

**Fig 5.3** To determine an Estimated Position (EP), apply leeway and tidal stream to the boat's course steered.

distance from position A along the water track. This is the distance the boat has travelled in 1 hour.

3. Apply the tidal stream from this mark in the direction of 170°T for a distance of 1 mile measured from the latitude scale. This is the distance the tidal stream has travelled in 1 hour.
4. Mark this end position with the symbol for an estimated position (EP).

## Log

The log is an instrument that measures speed or distance travelled through the water. The log reading is the distance travelled as indicated by the log.

SYMBOLS

DR (Dead Reckoning Position) +

EP (Estimated Position) Δ

Fix (Position determined from observation) ☉

# QUESTION PAPER 5 – WHAT IS THE POSITION?

Answers on page 181–2                                    All times are BST

5.1   At 1030 a boat is 2 miles west of Varne Lightvessel. She steers a course of 320°T speed 3 knots. Tidal stream is slack and there is no leeway. What is her DR position at 1200?

5.2   At 0200, a boat in DR position 51° 2′·6N, 1° 16′·5E log reading 98·4, steers a course of 255°T. For the next 2 hours, wind is northerly, leeway estimated as 10°, there is no tidal stream. What is the DR position at 0400 when the log reading was 106·4?

5.3   At 0935, a boat is in EP 50° 53′·2N, 1° 4′·0E steering a course of 274°T at a speed of 4 knots. Leeway is 5° due to a southerly wind. At 0935 it is 5 hours before HW Dover, neap tides. What is the EP at 1135? (Use tidal diamond E, practice chart 5055. See page 76 for an explanation of tidal diamonds.)

## Chapter Six

# A Course to Steer

## The Effects Of Tidal Stream And Leeway

In the absence of any leeway or tidal stream, the course to steer between two places would be the direction of a straight line (track) drawn on the chart between them. This line is drawn on the chart and is called the ground track. If the ground track is to be maintained, then a course must be steered to counteract the effects of tidal stream and leeway.

This is achieved by altering course into the tidal stream and wind.

EXAMPLE 10

It is required to determine the course to steer from position A to position B in fig 6 counteracting a tidal stream of 135°T 1 knot and 5° leeway caused by a northerly wind. The boat's speed is 4 knots and the bearing of B from A is 080°T.

1. A line is drawn from position A to position B. This is the desired ground track and is marked with 2 arrowheads for identification.
2. The set and drift of the tidal stream for a period of 1 hour is applied to A. This line is marked with 3 arrowheads (1 mile 135°T).
3. The boat's speed over a period of 1 hour is applied next by measuring the distance travelled (4 miles), from the end of the line representing the tidal stream C and striking an arc across the ground track D.
4. A line is drawn from C to D, and this is the true direction of the course to steer counteracting the tidal stream (068°T); it is marked with 1 arrowhead. This line is the water track.
5. The 5° leeway is then applied to the water track. This is applied into wind giving a course to steer of 063°T. To convert this true course to a compass course to steer variation and deviation must be applied.

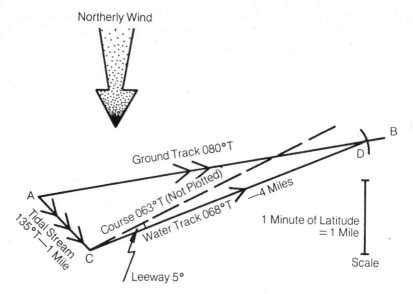

**Fig 6** Finding the course to steer. To sail from A to B, this helmsman must initially steer 063°T, as explained in Example 10. This brings him to point D after one hour, after which he must repeat the calculation, taking into account any changes in the tidal stream and leeway, for the remainder of the passage.

### LEEWAY

Leeway would be checked in the first five minutes by observation of the direction of the water track relative to the fore and aft line of the boat.

### VECTORS

The lines forming the plot are called vectors, and the construction formed by these vectors is called a vector diagram or triangle (fig 6). This has only been plotted for the first hour, and to reach the destination B a further small triangle would have to be made if any of the factors had changed within that hour: boat speed, tidal stream, leeway.

Although the boat's speed was 4 knots through the water, the speed made good over the ground between A and D (4·5 knots) is more than this, because the tidal stream has been pushing the boat along.

### SYMBOLS

Water track    ———→———

Ground track ———»———

Drift           ———»»»———

# QUESTION PAPER 6 – A COURSE TO STEER

Answers on page 181

All times are BST

6.1 (a) What is the true course from a position 50° 49'·2N, 0° 38'·6E to a position 2 miles south of Dungeness Point, assuming there is no tidal stream and no leeway?
(b) If the boat's speed is 5 knots, how long will it take to travel the distance between these two positions (to the nearest minute)?

6.2 (a) Using the same two positions, find the true course, allowing for a tidal stream of 118°T 2·2 knots and 5° leeway due to a south easterly wind. The tidal stream is constant throughout this problem.
(b) What is the EP after two hours?
(c) If the boat started at 0750, what is the estimated time of arrival (ETA) 2 miles south of Dungeness Point?
(d) What is the speed made good?

6.3 (a) Plot the true course from a position at 1600 2 miles south of Vergoyer SW buoy (50° 26'·9N, 1° 0'·0E) to position 50° 35'·2N, 1° 3'·0E. The wind is north easterly, leeway 10°, boats speed 4 knots.
(b) What is the ETA?

### Tidal Streams

| Time | Dir | Rate |
|------|------|------|
| 1600–1700 | 062°T | 2·2 knots |
| 1700–1800 | 092°T | 2·3 knots |
| 1800–1900 | 130°T | 2·0 knots |

*Chapter Seven*

# Position Lines

Conditions do not remain constant throughout a passage. There may have been an incorrect estimation of the tidal stream or leeway, the speed may have varied, or the helmsman may not have kept a steady course. It is necessary, therefore, for the navigator to check the boat's position frequently (at least every half hour), and if necessary to re-plot the course.

When the boat's position is found by taking two or more bearings, or by taking a bearing and intersecting it with a position line found by some other method, the position is called a fix. Given accurate bearings it is a precise method of position finding because no allowance has to be made for tidal stream or wind.

### Plotting Position Lines

A line obtained by taking a bearing is called a position line (P/L). A single line gives one piece of information only: that the boat is somewhere along it. To find the actual position along that line it is necessary to intersect it with further position lines from one or more additional bearings. It is not necessary to plot position lines all the way from the chosen objects as this will quickly clutter up the chart; simply plot the small portion of the line at the intersection (Fig 7.1). The time when the fix was taken and the log reading, in brackets, are written next to the fix as a useful record for later reference. A fix is marked with a dot in a circle.

Not all objects are suitable to use for taking bearings, and the following points should be considered:

1. If two bearings are taken, the angle of cut between the position lines obtained from them should be between 70° and 110° (ideally 90°), and if three bearings are taken the angle between any two should be between 30° and 150° (ideally 60°). Bearings which differ much from these requirements will not give reliable results, because the narrow angle of cut means that the smallest variation in bearing may shift the point of intersection by several miles.

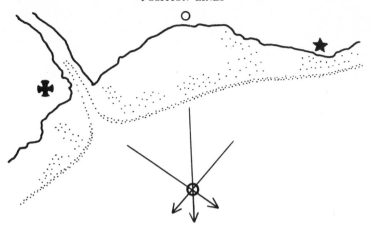

**Fig 7.1** A plotted position fix from bearings on three objects. The intersection is rarely so accurate as this.

2. The chosen objects must be easily identified without ambiguity both visually and on the chart.
3. Headlands and land features which merge with the background can often be misleading.
4. Buoys should be used with caution, because they shift their position with tidal movement and they can drag their moorings or easily be wrongly identified.
5. The nearer the objects chosen the better, as there is less likelihood of error.
6. Bearings abeam of the boat should be taken last as they will alter more quickly than those ahead or astern.
7. A spot height, though it appears on the chart, is often difficult to identify from sea level, and therefore should not normally be used.

COCKED HAT

It is unusual for three position lines to intersect perfectly, and normally a small triangle or cocked hat is formed. (See Fig 7.2) If a large cocked hat is present the bearings should be checked, as the probability of being inside it is small. Errors may have been caused for the following reasons:

1. Lack of accuracy when taking the bearing, especially in heavy weather when it is difficult to hold the hand bearing compass steady.
2. Bad plotting.
3. Application of variation the wrong way.
4. Wrong identification of one of the objects.
5. The distance the boat has travelled between taking the bearings.

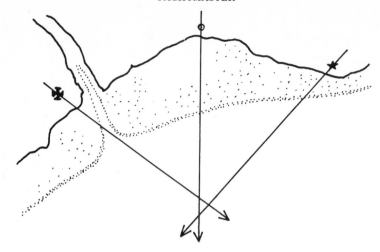

**Fig 7.2** A 'cocked hat' triangle is usually formed by three bearings taken, due to minor inaccuracy in taking the bearings. You should not necessarily assume that your actual position lies within the cocked hat. For clarity, the lines of position are here shown as being drawn all the way from the objects, but when plotting you should keep the drawn line as short as possible.

6. Magnetic deviation due to holding the hand bearing compass near to anything which will affect it, such as the rigging.

A TRANSIT

A transit is the name used when two objects are in line. It gives the most accurate position line possible, and a course can be steered along it without reference to the steering compass; Fig 7.3.

A LINE OF SOUNDINGS

If there is some method of obtaining the depth, and there is a prominent feature on the sea bed, the boat can run a line of soundings recording the depth of water below her at intervals. Before the results obtained can be compared with the figures on the chart, an allowance has to be made for the height of water above chart datum (see Chapter 8) at that particular time.

The corrected figures can be plotted on tracing paper, which can then be moved around the area concerned until the figures on the chart and on the tracing paper coincide.

It may be possible to locate a seabed contour line and take a bearing at the same time, but the position found by this method should be regarded with caution, as soundings will give, at best, only a rough idea of position unless the seabed has an unmistakable feature by which to identify it.

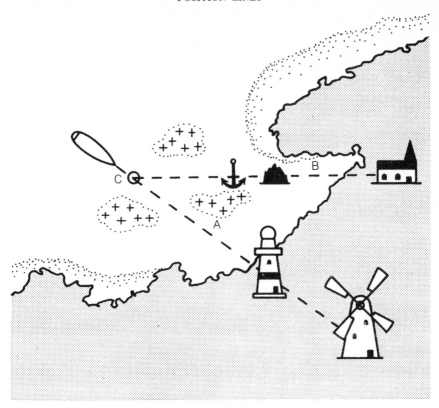

**Fig 7.3** Transits. More than one transit can be used at a time, either in succession to pilot the boat into harbour (line A and then line B); or at the same time to fix your position (point C).

## A Running Fix

Also called a transferred position line. This is a useful method when only one position line can be obtained at a particular time; Fig 7.4. The procedure is as follows:

1. Take the first bearing and plot the position line. Note the time and log reading. The boat is somewhere along this line.
2. Run on for a reasonable distance so that a good angle of cut will be obtained when a second bearing of the same object is taken. Keep a steady course and speed and note the distance run, so that the water track is known.
3. Take a second bearing and plot the position line. Note the time and log reading. Obviously the boat is along this line also, but at the moment, it is not known where.
4. From any point along the first position line, preferably near the DR or

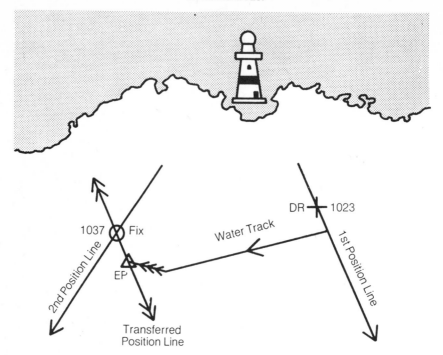

**Fig 7.4** The transferred position line, which should be plotted with double arrowheads at each end.

EP, lay off the water track and plot the distance travelled along it during the period between bearings.

5. At the end of this distance, lay off the drift due to tidal stream equivalent to the distance travelled. This is the EP.

6. Using the parallel rule, draw a line through the EP parallel to the first position line. This is the transferred position line (marked with two arrowheads on each end for identification). Where it intersects the second position line is the fix.

7. Write the time and log reading by the fix.

The accuracy of this method relies upon the correct estimation of leeway and tidal stream, and upon maintaining a constant course and speed. It can be used with only one object, or with two objects when only one of them is visible at a time.

SINGLE POSITION LINE

A single position line can sometimes be used to steer the boat around obstructions; in Fig 7.5 the boat wishes to clear the obstruction and enter the port. The first bearing is taken of a convenient object ashore, and the distance from that bearing to a point opposite to the intended destination

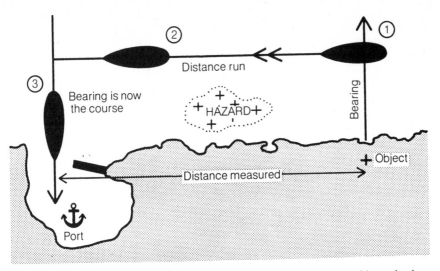

**Fig 7.5** Using a single position line to avoid a hazard when approaching a harbour.

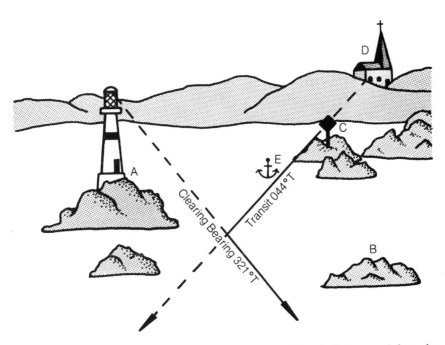

**Fig 7.6** A clearing bearing and a transit. When approaching the lit beacon A from the south east, its bearing must be kept above 321°T in order to avoid running up on rock B. Then the transit (church D in line with beacon C) guides you to anchorage at E.

is measured; this will be the distance the boat has to travel before turning. At the end of this distance the bearing is used as a course to enter the port, the boat having safely passed the obstruction. If there is any tidal stream or leeway this must, of course, be allowed for.

## Clearing Bearings

These are bearings used to clear hazards. Transits and clearing bearings are used extensively when entering port, and are often shown on the chart or described in the sailing directions. They are useful for clearing offlying obstructions or where there are obstructions on either side of the approach to the destination. Figure 7.6 shows clearing bearings to enable a boat to make a safe passage into the bay. Provided she keeps within these bearings she is safe. If a transit can be found instead of a bearing, this avoids constantly checking the compass.

## Useful Angles

The relationship between certain angles can sometimes be used to advantage for navigational purposes. The information obtained does not need to be plotted, this has only been done in the examples to illustrate the methods. Any convenient pair of angles can be used for the example; in Fig 7.7, 30° and 60° have been chosen.

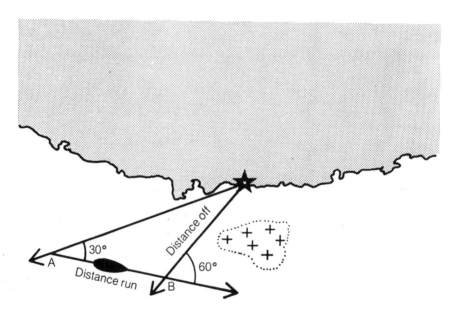

**Fig 7.7** Doubling the angle on the bow to find out the distance from a sighted object. When the angle is doubled, distance off equals distance run, on the principle of the isosceles triangle.

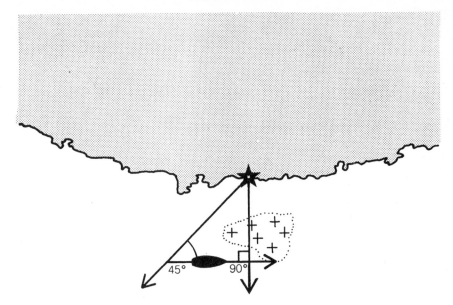

**Fig 7.8** The dangers of using 45° and 90° for obtaining distance off by doubling the angle on the bow: by the time the object sighted is abeam, the boat may have arrived at the offlying danger.

The angle between the boat's head and the object is noted as a relative bearing; the log reading is noted at the same time. The boat continues on the same course until the angle between the boat's head and the object has doubled. The distance travelled (measured by log), equals the distance the boat is off the object at the time of the second bearing, because she has sailed along one of the equal sides of an isosceles traingle, the distance off being the other equal side.

A variation of this is to use the angles 45° and 90°, which form a right angled triangle and so give the distance off when the object is abeam; see Fig 7.8. The results will be more accurate because the angles are broader than in the first example. The disadvantage of this particular pair of angles, however, is that the boat will be abeam before the distance off is known, whereas the previous method gives the distance off before the boat reaches this point thus, if the object of the exercise is to avoid an offlying hazard, the first method is preferable.

Both these methods rely upon the distance over the land and the course being accurate and they cannot be used in strong tidal stream situations.

## Sextant Angles

The sextant is an instrument used for measuring the angle subtended at the observer between two objects, by superimposing a mirror image onto an actual object. It is widely used in celestial navigation for taking sights of heavenly bodies, but also used for coastal navigation to obtain angles between terrestial objects.

VERTICAL SEXTANT ANGLE

The vertical angle subtended by an object of known height enables the distance off the object to be found, either by consulting a set of nautical tables, or by using the formula:

$$\text{Distance off in miles} = \frac{\text{Height of the object in metres} \times 1{\cdot}854}{\text{Vertical sextant angle in minutes}}$$

The tables and formula are based upon the relationship between an angle, the base and the perpendicular of a right angled triangle; given the perpendicular and the angle, the base can be determined.

EXAMPLE 11

Beachy Head Light, height 25m, VSA 7° 31′ = 451′

$$\frac{25 \times 1{\cdot}854}{451} = 0{\cdot}1 \text{ (mile)}$$

We know from this calculation that we are 0·1 miles from Beachy Head Light, but we do not know in which direction, because our answer has given us a position circle not a position line. To find out our exact position we will need another position circle or else a bearing of Beachy Head Light.

In order to measure the angle subtended by the top and bottom of a

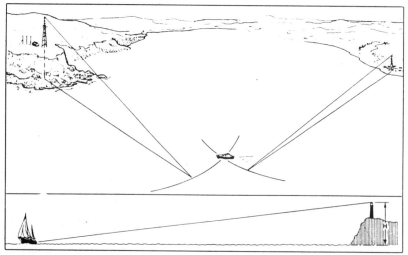

**Fig 7.9** Vertical sextant angles from two objects give a fix where the arcs cut.

landmark of known elevation (which on British charts is always measured above the level of Mean High Water Springs), it is necessary to have a clear view of the sea level beneath the chosen object, which means that a small boat with a low elevation will need to be fairly close to the shore. Ideally an allowance for tide should be made; if this is not done the position circle will appear to be further away from the object than it really is, but the level of high water can often be detected as a tidemark on cliffs or rocks.

If it is required to stay a certain distance offshore, the angle for that distance can be found and set on the sextant. Provided this safety angle does not increase, the boat stays at or outside the required distance (the nearer the object the greater the angle).

HORIZONTAL SEXTANT ANGLE

If the sextant is turned so that it is held horizontally, it can be used to measure the angle subtended at the observer between two shore objects. A distance off is not obtained from a horizontal angle as from a vertical angle, but a position circle can be plotted. Two such circles can be obtained from three landmarks; where they intersect is the fix. There are several methods of constructing a position circle, two of which are shown:

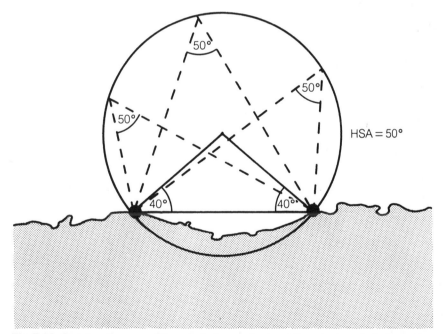

**Fig 7.10** Constructing a position circle from a horizontal sextant angle between two objects of 50°, using method 1. The boat is somewhere on the circumference.

*Method 1 (Fig 7.10)*
1. Draw a base line between the two objects, joining them together.
2. If the angle measured on the sextant is less than 90°, take it from 90° and lay off the resultant angle from each end of the base line on the same side as the boat.
3. If the angle measured is greater than 90°, take 90° from it and lay off the resultant angle from the base line on the opposite side to the boat.
4. The lines laid off from the base line intersect at the centre of the circle. The radius of the circle is from the centre to either object. The circle can now be drawn.

*Method 2 (Fig 7.11)*
1. Draw a line joining the objects (AB).
2. Bisect this with a perpendicular (CD).
3. From A lay off the angle measured with the sextant (AE).
4. Perpendicular to line AE at A draw a line (AF).
5. Where AF intersects CD is the centre of the circle, the radius is from the centre to A or B.

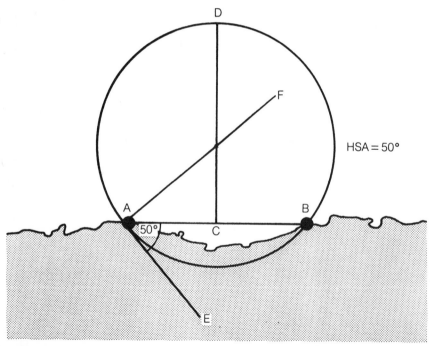

**Fig 7.11** Constructing a position circle from a horizontal sextant angle between two objects, using method 2.

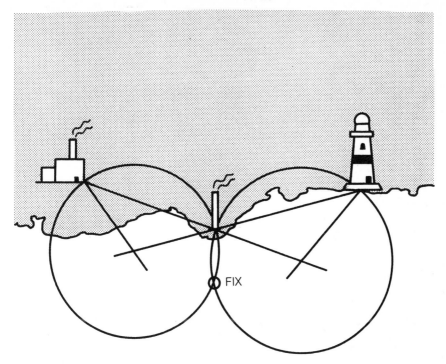

**Fig 7.12** Two horizontal sextant angles on three objects give a fix where the circles intersect.

Figure 7.12 shows two position circles, the point of intersection being the fix.

When the three objects chosen are all on a circle which passes through the boat, then only one position circle can be obtained. Therefore choose objects which are along a straight line, where the middle object is nearer than the other two, or where the boat is inside a circle formed by the three objects.

### Using Compass Bearings

As an alternative to using horizontal sextant angles, the angular difference between bearings may be used. This can be useful if it is desired to check the compass deviation. Whether the bearings taken are true, magnetic or compass, the angle between them will remain the same. When the position is found the true bearings can be compared with the compass bearings and, when variation has been applied, any remaining difference is deviation.

SQUARE PROTRACTOR OR TRACING PAPER

The angles found either by sextant or compass can be drawn on a transparent square protractor or tracing paper.

Figure 7.13 shows a protractor with lines drawn either side of the centre north line (marked with an N). The angles between these lines are 59° and 77° which were obtained from three bearings: 322°, 021° 098°. To find the boat's position, the protractor is placed on the chart with the centre line on the middle object, and moved around until the other two lines cut through the objects either side of the central one. A pencil or pin is pushed through the hole in the middle of the protractor to mark the fix. The tracing paper is used in a similar manner, but the central line has to be drawn as well as the other two lines.

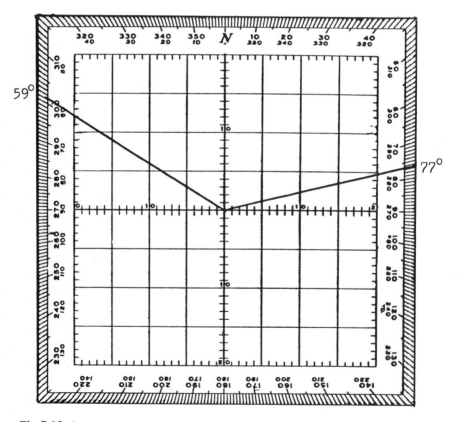

**Fig 7.13** A square protractor.

STATION POINTER

Another useful instrument when angles are used to find position, or three
bearings are to be plotted, is a station pointer. This is an instrument with
three arms (the middle one is fixed and the two outer ones pivot) attached
to a scale graduated in degrees. The arms are adjusted to the required
angles or bearings and the station pointer moved into position on the chart
in the same way as the marked square protractor.

SYMBOL

Transferred P/L   «————————»

# QUESTION PAPER 7 – POSITION FIXING

Answers on page 181 and 186–9.

7.1   The following bearings were taken from a boat in DR position
50° 52'·0N, 0° 53'·0E.
>                    Tower (20) (East of Camber Church) 351°C
>                    Tower (18) (2½ miles W of Dungeness lighthouse) 046°C
>                    Dungeness lighthouse 074°C

Variation is 6°W, plot the position.
>        (a)  What is the depth?
>        (b)  What is the deviation?

7.2   A boat to the east of Folkestone takes a VSA of 3° 46'·0 between the
HW line at the bottom of Shakespeare Cliff and the top of the radio masts.
The bearing of the radio masts was 340°T.
>        (a)  What is the position?
>        (b)  What is the depth of water?

7.3   At 1245, a boat on a course of 332°T takes a bearing of Pt du Touquet
light (50° 32'·0N, 1° 35'·5E) of 070°T. At 1345 the same light bore 105°T.
Boat's speed was 5 knots, leeway 10° due to an easterly wind, tidal stream
265°T, 2 knots. What is the 1345 position?

7.4   Plot the following bearings:
>        South Goodwin lightvessel          050°T
>        Varne lightvessel                  165°T
>        Folkestone light Gp.Fl (2)         275°T

Do you think the fix obtained is satisfactory?

*Chapter Eight*

# Tides

Tide is a vertical movement of water which, around our coasts, happens twice in approximately 25 hours (called semi-diurnal tides). During this period two low waters and two high waters occur. In other parts of the world diurnal tides occur where there is only one low water and one high water each day.

Tides are caused by the gravitational field of the moon and to a lesser extent the sun. The effect of the moon's gravity upon the earth is not, however, uniform and the surface nearer the moon experiences a greater pull than the centre of the earth. This makes the water at this point move towards the moon faster than the earth itself, which is solid, and the oceans on that side bulge towards the moon. On the earth's other side the pull is weaker still and the water gets left slightly behind, bulging backwards.

The sun exerts a similar pull upon the oceans but, because it is much further away from the earth than the moon, the effect is not so great.

When the sun and moon are in line relative to the earth, their gravitational forces combine to cause the maximum tidal range called a spring tide, at which time the high water is higher and the low water lower than at other times.

When the sun and moon are at right angles relative to the earth, their forces on the earth are acting in opposition, and a minimum tidal range occurs. This is called a neap tide, in which the extremes of tide are less than at other times.

Spring tides occur shortly after new and full moon, and neap tides occur shortly after the quarter moon. During a lunar month, following the moon's cycle which is approximately 4 weeks, two spring tides and two neap tides will occur.

## Nomenclature

### EQUINOXES

Twice a year the sun is directly over the equator and at these times, especially if the moon is in line with the sun, larger than normal tides occur. The largest of these is called the Equinoctial Spring Tide which occurs twice a year on about 21st March (vernal equinox) and the 23rd September (autumnal equinox).

### CHART DATUM (CD)

Chart Datum is the level of the sea at or near the Lowest Astronomical Tide (LAT). For areas surveyed by the Hydrographer of the Navy, it is referred to the Ordnance Datum at Newlyn in Cornwall. LAT is the lowest level, taking into account astronomical conditions, to which the tide is expected to fall. Normally the sea will be above that level but occasionally, when affected by high barometric pressure, strong winds or storm surges, it may fall below it.

The depth of water below CD is shown on the sea area of the chart by figures indicating depth in metres and decimetres. For example, 3 metres would be shown as 3, and 3·8 metres as $3_8$ (on a fathom chart the figures will be in fathoms and feet).

### DRYING HEIGHT

If part of the sea bed, such as a rock or bank, projects above CD but is completely covered by the tide at high water, its height above CD will be indicated by a figure with a line drawn under it; drying 2 metres would be shown as 2.

### MEAN HIGH WATER SPRINGS (MHWS) MEAN LOW WATER SPRINGS (MLWS)

### MEAN HIGH WATER NEAPS (MHWN) MEAN LOW WATER NEAPS (MLWN)

These are the average of the heights above CD of all spring and neap high and low tides throughout the year. These mean levels are indicated on some coastal charts, in *Admiralty Tide Tables*, *Reed's Nautical Almanac* and other nautical publications.

### TIDAL RANGE

This is the difference in metres or feet between the height of high water and the preceding or succeeding low water. The difference in height between MHWS and MLWS is called the mean spring range, and the difference between MHWN and MLWN the mean neap range. If the range of any particular tide is compared with these ranges, it can be established whether the tide is springs, neaps or an intermediate tide (this information will be needed later for tidal calculations).

HIGH WATER AND LOW WATER (HW LW)

High water and low water are heights measured above CD

DURATION

This is the period of time between high and low water, for a falling tide, or between low water and high water for a rising tide.

RISE

The rise is the difference in height between any high water and CD.

HEIGHT

The height is the vertical difference between sea level and CD at any given time.

TIDAL CURVE

The change in sea level during a tidal cycle presented graphically in the Tide Tables.

## Calculations

TIMES AND HEIGHTS OF TIDE

The times and heights of high and low water for standard ports can be found by reference to the appropriate tide tables. Differences based on these standard ports are given for other places.

THE HEIGHT OF TIDE (THE TWELFTHS RULE)

The tide does not rise or fall at a constant rate throughout its duration. If the tidal curve for any particular port is symmetrical, a rule for a quick approximation of intermediate heights between high and low water can be used. This rule is called the rule of twelfths, and it is based on the assumption that the tide rises or falls as follows:

| Hour | Proportion of Tidal Range |
|------|---------------------------|
| 1st  | 1/12 |
| 2nd  | 2/12 |
| 3rd  | 3/12 |
| 4th  | 3/12 |
| 5th  | 2/12 |
| 6th  | 1/12 |

*Example 12*
The range is 4·8m and the duration 6 hours.

| Hours | Rise/Fall Range | Rise/Fall Hourly | Rise/Fall Total |
|-------|-----------------|------------------|-----------------|
| 1 | 1/12 | 0·4 | 0·4 |
| 2 | 2/12 | 0·8 | 1·2 |
| 3 | 3/12 | 1·2 | 2·4 |
| 4 | 3/12 | 1·2 | 3·6 |
| 5 | 2/12 | 0·8 | 4·4 |
| 6 | 1/12 | 0·4 | 4·8 |

The answer obtained by this method is only approximate and should be used with caution. It is of no use where the tidal curve is not symmetrical, such as the Solent where special methods are used. The height found is above LW.

ADMIRALTY TIDE TABLES (ATT)

These tables give HW and LW times, heights, and tidal curve diagrams for standard ports, the differences to apply to standard ports for secondary ports, together with seasonal corrections and supplementary tables. Some ports require a special method of calculation to be used, and these are marked with a 'c' accordingly; the procedure for these ports is fully explained in the Hydrographic publication *Simplified Harmonic Method of Tidal Prediction NP 159*. For offshore areas between secondary ports a co-tidal chart, which is self-explanatory, is available from the Hydrographic office.

STANDARD PORTS

*Example 13a:* **Finding a time for a given height**
At what time (BST) will the tide fall to a height of 3.3m at Dover during the afternoon of 22nd September?

Extract the relevant times and heights of high water and low water from the tide tables (correcting to local time as necessary) and work out the range:

| | HW | | LW | | Range |
|---|---|---|---|---|---|
| | Time | Height | Time | Height | |
| Dover | 0957 BST | 6.3m | 1737 BST | 1.1m | 5.2m (0.3 from springs) |

*Refer to Extract 1*
(1) Fill in the time scale at the bottom of the tidal curve with HW and hours before and after HW as required.
(2) Mark the HW height along the top height scale (H.W.Hts.m) and the LW height along the bottom height scale (L.W.Hts.m).
(3) Draw a range line between the LW mark and the HW mark.

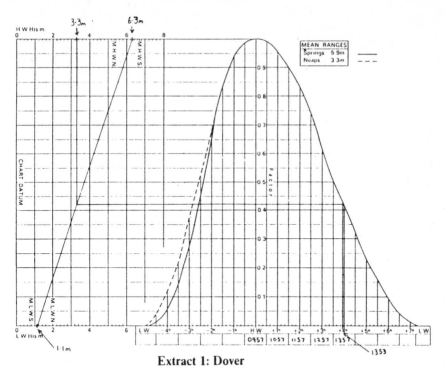

**Extract 1: Dover**

(4) Mark the height of tide required along the top height scale. Draw a vertical line downwards from this point to intersect the range line.

(5) From the point of intersection on the range line draw a horizontal line to the right to cut the rising or falling tidal curve as appropriate. Interpolation between the curves for spring and neap ranges is done visually (where appropriate) after comparing the predicted tidal range with the mean ranges for springs and neaps. (Do not extrapolate outside the spring and neap curves.)

(6) From the point of intersection on the tidal curve, draw a vertical line downwards to intersect the time scale and read off the time (1353).

*Example 13b:* **Finding a height for a given time**
What will be the height of tide at Dover at 2040 (BST) on 7th September?

Extract the relevant times and heights of high water and low water from the tide tables (correcting to local time as necessary) and work out the range:

|  | HW | | LW | | Range |
|---|---|---|---|---|---|
|  | Time | Height | Time | Height | |
| Dover | 2327 BST | 6.1m | 1809 BST | 1.2m | 4.9m (0.4 from springs) |

*Refer to Extract 2*

Proceed as for Example 13a as far as step (3).

(4) Enter the time scale with the required time and draw a vertical line upwards to the tidal curve, interpolating if necessary between spring and neap curves.

(5) From the point of intersection on the tidal curve draw a horizontal line to the left to inersect the range line.

(6) From the point of intersection on the range line draw a line vertically upwards to the top height scale and read off the height (3.1m).

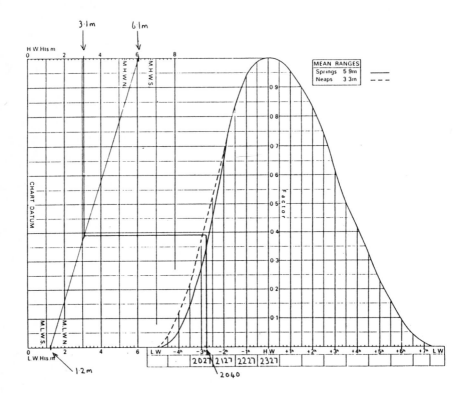

**Extract 2: Dover**

## SECONDARY PORTS

The HW and LW times and heights for secondary ports are found by applying the differences for that secondary port to the times and heights noted for the standard port.

If the required HW and LW time at the standard port falls between the times indicated at the head of the columns for the secondary differences, interpolation between the columns must be used. Refer to Extract 3 showing secondary differences under Dover. The HW difference for Folkstone would be −0020 minutes if the HW time at Dover was 0000 or 1200, or −0005 minutes if the time of HW at Dover was 0600 or 1800; the difference between these columns is 15 minutes. Therefore if the time of HW at Dover had been 0200, this would have been one third of the way between 0000 and 0600, and so one third of the difference (5 minutes) would have been subtracted from −0020, giving a difference at 0200 of −0015 minutes. Extrapolation is not used.

The HW and LW heights are obtained in a similar manner. The differences for heights at secondary ports are tabulated under the mean spring and mean neap heights for the standard port. Differences for intermediate HW and LW heights (at the secondary port) can be found by interpolation and extrapolation.

When the HW and LW times and heights for the secondary port have been obtained, the procedure for finding intermediate times and heights is the same as for standard ports. The standard port diagram is entered with secondary port times and heights unless there is a marked difference in the duration of rise and fall at the secondary port.

When there is not a suitable standard port, the letter 'p' replaces the time difference and the *Simplified Harmonic Method of Tidal Prediction NP 159* must be used.

See worked Example 14a and 14b on next two pages.

## ENGLAND, SOUTH COAST - DOVER

### LAT 51°07'N   LONG 1°19'E

TIME ZONE GMT

TIMES AND HEIGHTS OF HIGH AND LOW WATERS

| | SEPTEMBER | | | | OCTOBER | | | | NOVEMBER | | | | DECEMBER | |
|---|---|---|---|---|---|---|---|---|---|---|---|---|---|---|
| TIME | M | TIME | M | | TIME | M | TIME | M | | TIME | M | TIME | M | | TIME | M | TIME | M |

**7** 0448 1.4 **22** 0406 1.4 **7** 0518 1.3 **22** 0431 1.0 **7** 0546 1.3 **22** 0539 0.8 **7** 0549 1.3 **22** 0605 0.9
0957 6.2   0857 6.3   1010 6.4   0914 6.7   1045 6.6   1021 7.0   1052 6.5   1055 6.7
SU 1709 1.2 M 1637 1.1 TU 1734 1.2 W 1701 0.7 F 1800 1.2 SA 1807 0.6 SU 1808 1.1 M 1835 0.8
2227 6.1   2117 6.4   2235 6.3   2136 6.8   2306 6.5   2248 6.9   2315 6.5   2327 6.7

| | | | | | 0000 and 1200 | 0600 and 1800 | 0100 and 1300 | 0700 and 1900 | | | |
|---|---|---|---|---|---|---|---|---|---|---|---|
| 89 | DOVER | . | . | . | (see page 22) | 0000 and 1200 | 0600 and 1800 | 0100 and 1300 | 0700 and 1900 | 6·7 | 5·3 | 2·0 | 0·8 |
| 85 | Hastings | . | . | 50 51 | 0 35 | 0000 | −0010 | −0030 | −0030 | +0·8 | +0·5 | +0·1 | −0·1 |
| 86 | Rye (Approaches) | . | . | 50 55 | 0 47 | +0005 | −0010 | ⊙ | ⊙ | +1·0 | +0·7 | ⊙ | ⊙ |
| 86a | Rye (Harbour) | . | . | 50 56 | 0 46 | +0005 | −0010 | ⊙ | ⊙ | −1·4 | −1·7 | ⊙ | ⊙ |
| 87 | Dungeness | . | . | 50 54 | 0 58 | −0014 | −0014 | −0011 | −0021 | +1·3 | +1·0 | +0·3 | +0·2 |
| 88 | Folkestone | . | . | 51 05 | 1 12 | −0020 | −0005 | −0010 | −0010 | +0·4 | +0·4 | 0·0 | −0·1 |
| 89 | DOVER | . | . | 51 07 | 1 19 | STANDARD PORT | | | | | See Table V | | |
| 98 | Deal | . | . | 51 13 | 1 25 | +0010 | +0020 | +0010 | +0005 | −0·6 | −0·3 | 0·0 | 0·0 |
| 102 | Ramsgate | . | . | 51 20 | 1 25 | +0020 | +0020 | −0007 | −0007 | −1·8 | −1·5 | −0·8 | −0·4 |

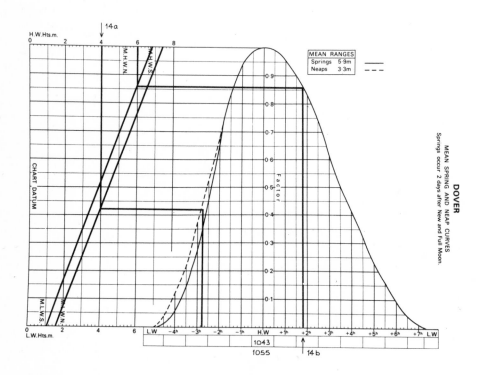

**Extract 3**

*Example 14a:* **Finding a time for a given height**
At what time (BST) will the tide rise to a height of 4.0m at Dungeness during
the morning of 7th September?

*Refer to Extract 3*

| *Standard Port* | Dover | | | | |
|---|---|---|---|---|---|
| | **HW** | | **LW** | | |
| | *Time* | *Height* | *Time* | *Height* | *Range* |
| *Dover* | 0957 GMT | 6.2m | 0448 GMT | 1.4m | 4.8m |
| *Difference* | −0014 | +1.2m | | +0.2m | (0.4 from |
| | 0943 GMT | 7.4m | | 1.6m | Springs) |
| *Dungeness* | 1043 BST | | | | |
| *Required height* | 4.0m | | | | |
| *Interval* | 2h 47m before HW | | | | |
| *HW Dungeness* | 1043 BST | | | | |
| *Time* | **0756 BST** | | | | |

*Example 14b*: **Finding a height for a given time**

What will be the height of tide at Folkestone at 1245 (BST) on 7th October?

*Refer to Extract 3*

| *Standard Port* | Dover | | | | |
|---|---|---|---|---|---|
| | **HW** | | **LW** | | |
| | *Time* | *Height* | *Time* | *Height* | *Range* |
| *Dover* | 1010 GMT | 6.4m | 1734 GMT | 1.2 | 5.2m |
| *Difference* | −0015 | +0.4m | | −0.1m | (0.2 from |
| | 0955 GMT | 6.8m | | 1.1m | Springs) |
| *Time* | 1055 BST | | | | |
| *Required* | 1245 BST | | | | |
| *Interval* | 1h 50m after HW | | | | |
| *HW Folkestone* | 1055 BST | | | | |
| *Height* | **6.0m** | | | | |

SWANAGE TO SELSEY

Complex tides occur in areas along the south coast of England between Swanage and Selsey due to shallow water effects. At some places these cause a stand of the tide for one or two hours, whilst at other places a second high water occurs. For these areas it is easier to calculate times and heights using LW as a reference, and special tidal curve diagrams are provided for this purpose. There are either two or three curves on each diagram, one for the spring range, one for the neap range, and sometimes one for a mid range. Where there are three curves, interpolation is between the mid curve and either the spring or the neap curve. The Portsmouth range defines the curve to use.

Where two high waters occur, the height of the higher one is used to find the range.

## ENGLAND, SOUTH COAST - PORTSMOUTH

LAT 50°48'N    LONG 1°07'W

TIME ZONE GMT                     TIMES AND HEIGHTS OF HIGH AND LOW WATERS

| MAY | | MAY | | JUNE | | JUNE | | JULY | | JULY | | AUGUST | | AUGUST | |
|---|---|---|---|---|---|---|---|---|---|---|---|---|---|---|---|
| TIME | M | TIME | M | TIME | M | TIME | M | TIME | M | TIME | M | TIME | M | TIME | M |
| **1** 0504 | 0.8 | **16** 0012 | 4.9 | **1** 0029 | 4.5 | **16** 0114 | 4.5 | **1** 0052 | 4.5 | **16** 0133 | 4.4 | **1** 0213 | 4.6 | **16** 0224 | 4.3 |
| 1207 | 4.4 | 0529 | 0.4 | 0548 | 0.7 | 0630 | 0.8 | 0616 | 0.7 | 0650 | 0.9 | 0739 | 0.5 | 0737 | 1.1 |
| TH 1720 | 0.8 | F 1240 | 4.8 | SU 1259 | 4.4 | M 1350 | 4.5 | TU 1328 | 4.5 | W 1407 | 4.5 | F 1453 | 4.8 | SA 1449 | 4.4 |
| | | 1749 | 0.6 | 1807 | 0.9 | 1849 | 1.2 | 1838 | 0.9 | 1909 | 1.2 | 2001 | 0.8 | 1957 | 1.3 |

| No. | PLACE | Lat. N. | Long. W. | High Water | | Low Water (Zone G.M.T.) | | MHWS | MHWN | MLWN | MLWS |
|---|---|---|---|---|---|---|---|---|---|---|---|
| | | | | TIME DIFFERENCES | | | | HEIGHT DIFFERENCES (IN METRES) | | | |
| 65 | **PORTSMOUTH** . . | (see page 14) | | 0000 and 1200 | 0600 and 1800 | 0500 and 1700 | 1100 and 2300 | 4·7 | 3·8 | 1·8 | 0·6 |
| 38 | Christchurch . . (Entrance) | 50 43 | 1 45 | −0230 | +0030 | −0035 | −0035 | −2.9 | −2·4 | −1·2 | −0·2 |

*Example 15a*  *Refer to Extract 4*
*Standard Port*      Portsmouth

|  | HW | | LW | | |
|---|---|---|---|---|---|
| | *Time* | *Height* | *Time* | *Height* | *Range* |
| *Portsmouth* | 1449 GMT | 4.4m | 1957 GMT | 1.3m | 3.1m |
| *Difference* | | 2.7m | −0035 | −0.8m | (between |
| *Christchurch* | | 1.7m | 1922 GMT | 0.5m | Spring and |
| | | | 2022 BST | | mid curve) |

*Required height*  1.2m
*Interval*          2h 30m before LW
*LW Christchurch*  2022 BST
*Time*              **1752 BST**

*Example 15 b*  *Refer to Extract 5*
*Standard Port*      Portsmouth

|  | HW | | LW | | |
|---|---|---|---|---|---|
| | *Time* | *Height* | *Time* | *Height* | *Range* |
| *Portsmouth* | 1350 GMT | 4.5m | 1847 GMT | 1.2m | 3.3m |
| *Difference* | | −2.8m | −0035 | −0.7m | (between |
| *Christchurch* | | 1.7m | 1814 GMT | 0.5m | Spring and |
| | | | 1914 GMT | | mid curve) |

*Required time*    1640 BST
*Interval*          2h 34m before LW
*LW Christchurch*  1914 BST
*Height*            **1.2m**

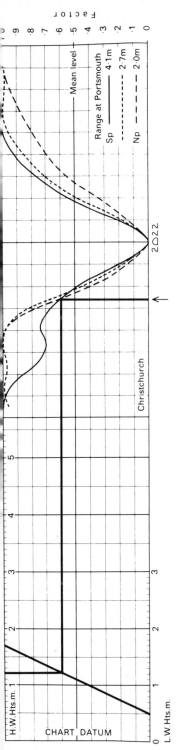

**Extract 4**

*Example 15a:* **Finding a time for a given height**
At what time (BST) will the tide fall to a height of 1.2m at Christchurch during
the afternoon of 16th August?

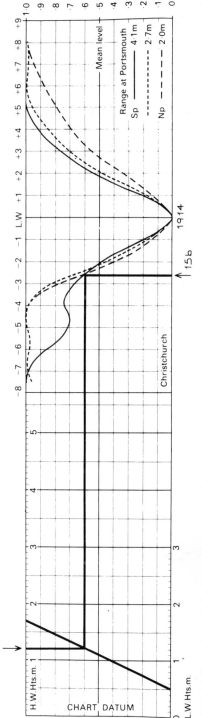

**Extract 5**

*Example 15b:* **Finding a height for a given time**
What will be the height of tide at Christchurch Harbour entrance at 1640 BST
on 16th June?

HEIGHTS OF OBJECTS ABOVE SEA LEVEL

These are referred to MHWS level to be compatible with heights shown on land maps; Fig 8.1 refers.

Sometimes it is necessary to calculate the amount the sea is below the MHWS level and thus find the height of the object above sea level. This is done in the following manner: The height of the object above MHWS is added to the MHWS height (found in ATT and on larger scale charts), thus finding the height of the object above CD. The height of tide above CD for the required time is found and subtracted from the height of the object above CD. The resultant answer is the height of the object above sea level.

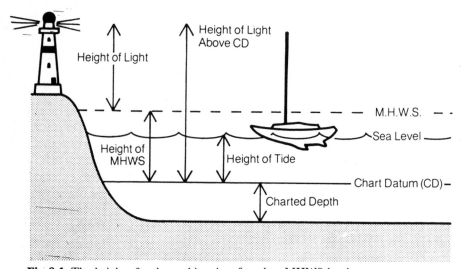

**Fig 8.1** The height of a shore object is referred to MHWS level.

*Example 16*

|  |  |
|---|---|
| Height of the light | 10m (above MHWS) |
| Height of MHWS | + 6m |
| | |
| Height of the light above CD | 16m |
| Height of the tide above CD | – 4m |
| | |
| Height of the light above sea level | 12m |

## Tidal Streams

### SURFACE CURRENTS

Surface currents are usually caused by the wind blowing along the surface of the sea, and should not be confused with the horizontal movement of water caused by astronomical forces (tidal streams). The tidal streams around the British Isles are usually stronger than the surface currents and so these are masked, but occasionally, after strong winds, they will be noticed in certain areas. They will vary, of course, with wind direction.

**Fig 8.2** A good look at anchored vessels, buoys etc will enable you to estimate the speed and direction of the tidal stream.

### TIDE RACES AND OVERFALLS

Tide races are caused by a land area, such as Portland Bill, extending into the tidal stream. Overfalls are caused by the tidal stream crossing shoaling waters. Both of these can be dangerous, especially at spring tides and in bad weather.

It is sometimes possible to pass inshore of a tide race, using the tidal stream to help the boat round the headland, but often it is necessary to go well out to sea to avoid a race or overfall.

### CONTRARY STREAMS

Inshore in a bay, there is often slacker water or even a contrary tidal stream which can be used to advantage if there is a foul tide further offshore.

ESTIMATING DIRECTION· AND SPEED OF TIDAL STREAMS

Observations of buoys, beacons, anchored vessels and river piles give a good indication of the direction and speed of tidal streams. Before mooring, it is wise to go past the mooring and make such an observation.

TIDAL DIAMONDS

The direction and rate (both spring and neap) of tidal flow are tabulated on charts at hourly intervals, referred to high water for the standard port for the chart concerned. This data is keyed to a specific position on the chart using a diamond symbol enclosing a letter corresponding to one of the tables. The tabulated data applies only to the hour shown and interpolation is necessary for intermediary times. This should not be done by using an arithmetic mean (unless the direction of the tidal stream is constant or nearly so) but by using a proportion of the hourly tabulation dependent on the time interval from the mean time of the tidal stream to be plotted.

*Example 17*

| W   Hours | Dir | Rate | |
| --- | --- | --- | --- |
| | | Sp | Np |
| Before HW  3 | 206° | 2.8 | 1.5 |
| 2 | 207° | 1.6 | 0.8 |
| 1 | 053° | 0.4 | 0.2 |
| After HW  HW | 040° | 1.8 | 1.0 |
| 1 | 035° | 2.3 | 1.3 |

The tidal stream sets towards the direction shown. The rate is in knots.

High Water (HW) at the standard port is at 1230 and it is a spring tide. it is desired to plot the tidal stream (in the vicinity of tidal diamond W) from 1115 to 1325.

The mean time between 1200 and 1300 is 1230, which corresponds with HW, so that the set and drift of the tidal stream between 1200 and 1300 is 040° 1.8 nautical miles. Between 1100 and 1200 the set and drift would be 053° 0.4 nautical miles (corresponding to a mean time of 1130, which is 1 hour before HW). The period required (from 1115 to 1200) is 45 minutes, so the drift will be $45/60 \times 0.4 = 0.3$ nautical miles. Similarly from 1300 to 1325 the set will be 035° and the drift $25/60 \times 2.3 = 1.0$ nautical miles.

So the tidal vectors to be plotted are:

1115–1200     053°   0.3M
1200–1300     040°   1.8M
1300–1325     035°   1.0M

For periods between springs and neaps it is necessary to interpolate between the tabulated rates.

# QUESTION PAPER 8 – TIDES

Extracts on pages 70, 72 and 73                         Answers on page 189

8.1    What height of tide will a boat, drawing 2.1m and requiring a clearance of 0.5m, need to cross a bar at Rye? The least depth on the bar has a drying height of 1.5m.

8.2    (a)  What are the times (BST) and heights of HW and LW at Portsmouth on 16th July?
       (b)  What are the ranges of the falling tides?
       (c)  Are they spring or neap tides?

8.3    What is the height of tide at Dover on 22nd September at 2015 BST?

8.4    What is the height above CD of the upper light at Dungeness?

8.5    What is the height of tide at Christchurch entrance on 16th May at 0400 BST?

8.6    At what time (GMT) will the height of tide reach 4.0m at Ramsgate on the evening of 7th November?

## Chapter Nine

# Weather to Sail

## Importance of Weather

Before any coastal or offshore passage is undertaken, it is extremely important to study the present and forthcoming weather. The important factors to consider are the strength and direction of the wind and the associated sea state, the length of time the wind has been blowing from one direction, the tidal stream in relation to the wind (seas are calmer when the wind and tidal stream are together, and a passage may be possible under these conditions, whereas with the turn of the tide an unpleasant situation can develop), and visibility.

No guide can be given as to when a boat should stay in port; this depends upon the type, size and seaworthiness of that boat, the capabilities and experience of the skipper and crew and the length of the passage. If in any doubt the wise skipper stays in port.

## Air Masses

In various parts of the world there are semi-permanent high pressure systems. Air moves outward from these systems to areas of lower pressure but, as this movement is relatively slow, the air has time to develop the surface characteristics of its source region. If this source region is situated at the poles the air mass will be cold. If on the other hand it is in sub-tropical latitudes it will be warm. It will also be dry or more humid dependent upon whether the source region is over land or sea. Further modifications to the air mass take place (in the lower levels) as it travels over different surfaces.

The main air masses reaching the British Isles are shown below:

### ARCTIC AND POLAR MARITIME

Cold at source, warmed from below as they travel over warmer seas. They are associated with cumulus and cumulo-nimbus cloud, showers and squalls.

POLAR CONTINENTAL

Cold at source and dry in the upper air, bringing very cold and often cloudy weather in winter.

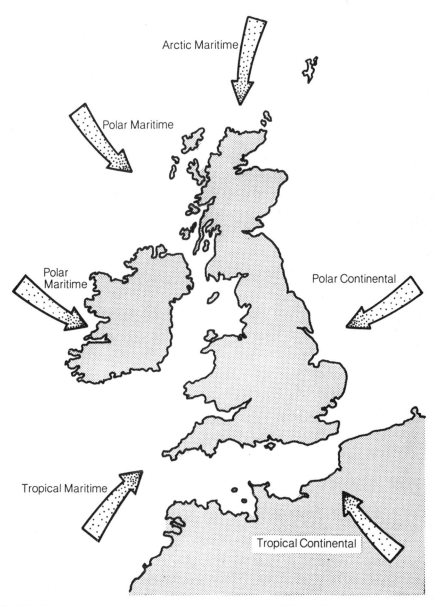

**Fig 9.1** The tracks of the main air masses reaching the British Isles.

TROPICAL MARITIME

Warm and moist at source and picks up moisture during its journey across the sea bringing cloud, rain or drizzle and fog.

TROPICAL CONTINENTAL

Warm and dry at source bringing warm usually cloudless conditions and possibly haze.

## Polar Front

When two air masses with different characteristics meet, they do not mix readily, and the line where they meet is called a Front. The boundary between polar and tropical air masses is called a Polar Front.

## A Depression (A Low Pressure System)

When conditions are favourable, a ripple may develop on the polar front and a depression forms distorting the polar front which is now re-named warm front or cold front, see Fig 9.2. Pressure in the centre falls as warm air rises and air from areas of higher pressure flows in to replace it. Because

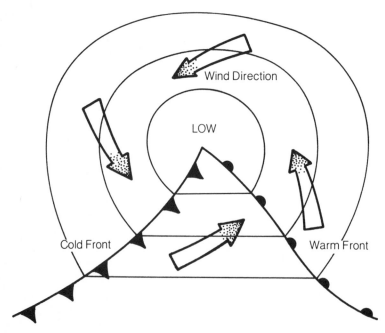

**Fig 9.2** A typical depression in the northern hemisphere.

of the earth's rotation, an anticlockwise circulation develops around the centre of the depression (in the northern hemisphere) as inflowing air is deflected to the right of its track.

Areas of equal pressure are joined together by lines called isobars. The ratio between the pressure difference and the distance between the isobars is the pressure gradient. In an intense depression, the isobars will be close together with strong winds, but in a weak depression the isobars will be spaced further apart with lighter winds.

BUYS BALLOT'S LAW

A simple way to determine the position of the centre of a depression in the northern hemisphere, is to stand with your back to the wind and the centre is on your left hand side.

## Weather Indications

The visual signs are very important to the mariner who, as well as listening to and studying the weather reports, should be aware of and able to make use of the changes occurring around him. Cloud observation is of prime importance because clouds often warn of approaching weather systems, especially depressions. A series of observations should be made over several days and the information backed up with other indications such as barometric trend.

The order in which cloud formations occur during the approach and passage of a typical depression is as follows (Fig 9.3):

WARM FRONT

| | |
|---|---|
| *Cirrus (Ci)* | Thread-like delicate clouds high up in the sky, still fine, visibility good. |
| *Cirrostratus (Cs)* | A veil-like covering lower than cirrus, giving the sky a misty appearance, visibility still good. |
| *Altostratus (As)* | A layer of cloud thicker and lower than cirrostratus giving a dull effect, visibility starts to deteriorate with possibly frontal rain or fog. |
| *Nimbostratus (Ns)* | Very thick and sombre looking layer cloud low in the sky. Visibility deteriorates further in heavier rain. |
| *Fractostratus (Fs)* | Broken off pieces flying along under the nimbostratus. |

On the passage of the warm front, layer cloud (stratus) is often present, but at the end nearest the cold front, cumulus appears. There may be rain or snow.

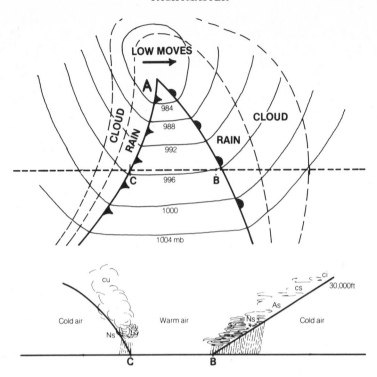

**Fig 9.3** As the depression centred at A moves across from left to right, observer at B sees the surface wind veer from S through SW to W as the warm front passes over; and observer at C sees the surface wind veer from W to NW as the cold front passes over.

COLD FRONT

| | |
|---|---|
| *Cumulus (Cu)* | Large cauliflower shaped clouds of great vertical height. |
| *Cumulonimbus (Cb)* | Cumulus rain cloud of great vertical height spreading out into an anvil shape. This can reach 12,000m and bring heavy rain, snow, hail or sleet. There can also be thunder and lightning. Visibility deteriorates during precipitation and frontal fog can occur. |

After the passage of a cold front there is a dramatic improvement in visibility, rain stops and skies clear, although there may be showers later.

TEMPERATURE

Rises slightly before the warm front, rises on the passage, remains constant in the warm sector and falls as the cold front passes.

BAROMETRIC TREND

The barometer falls at the approach of the warm front, stays steady in the warm sector, unless the depression is deepening when it will fall further, and rises on the passage of the cold front.

WIND

Backs and increases as the warm front approaches, veers on the passage of the front and remains fairly constant in the warm sector, usually backs a little as the cold front approaches and veers as the front passes.

AN OCCLUSION

Because of strong winds behind the cold front, it travels faster than the warm front, eventually catching it up and lifting the air in the warm sector upwards. When this happens the system has occluded and it will die out and disappear. The isobars at an occluded front develop a sharp angle and squally conditions can be present.

## An Anticyclone (A High Pressure System)

This is an area of high pressure with wind flowing out from its centre in a clockwise direction (in the northern hemisphere). Isobars are round or oval shaped and winds usually light. In summer the weather is usually good, but in winter the lack of wind and low surface temperature may allow pollution fog to persist.

## Fog

### DEW POINT

The temperature of air determines the amount of water vapour it can hold; the higher the temperature the more it can hold. When it is holding all the water vapour possible for a given temperature, it is termed saturated. The point at which this occurs is called dew point and, if the air is cooled below this dew point, condensation will occur which, if conditions are right, will be in the form of fog.

### RADIATION FOG

This forms by cooling of the ground at night after a relatively warm day especially if there is a clear sky when much heat is lost by radiation. If the layer of air in contact with the ground is cooled below its dew point then fog can form (Fig 9.4).

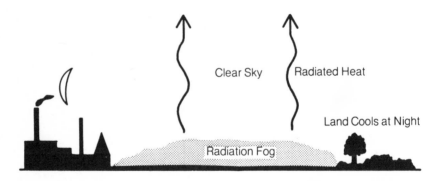

**Fig 9.4** Radiation fog forming at night. This forms over land, but can then drift out to sea for several miles.

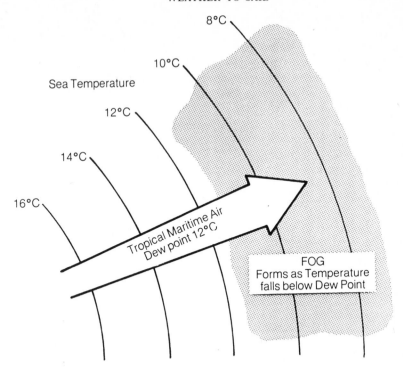

8°C

10°C

Sea Temperature

12°C

14°C

16°C

Tropical Maritime Air
Dew point 12°C

FOG
Forms as Temperature
falls below Dew Point

**Fig 9.5** Advection fog or sea fog forms when an air mass passes over sea which is colder than the air mass's dew point. It can occur in winds of up to Force 6.

In summer, day temperatures are often high and nights are short so fog is not frequent, but in winter the air may be quite near its dew point during the day, and the nights are cold and long, so fog occurs more often. Occasionally the air is so calm that continuous deposition of dew occurs, and the cooling does not extend through a layer of air and so no fog forms. At other times the wind persists overnight and the cooling extends upwards throughout the lower layer of air by turbulence, and stratus cloud forms. This type of fog forms over land but can drift out to sea for several miles.

ADVECTION FOG

This type of fog occurs in an air mass when it passes over sea colder than the air mass dew point. It can occur over land, but this is relatively rare because usually the resulting turbulence, greater overland, lifts it into stratus cloud if the wind is force 3 or more. Friction and therefore turbulence is much less over the sea (even if there are waves these are moving with the wind) and so fog can still occur in winds up to force 6. (Fig 9.5)

## Land and Sea Breezes

During the late forenoon (1030–1200) if the sun has warmed the land sufficiently, air in contact with the land is warmed and rises, being replaced by air flowing in from over the sea. This is a sea breeze and will persist as long as the sun is warm enough to warm the land sufficiently for the air to rise.

After sunset, the land cools, the air becomes heavier and rolls back towards the sea, displacing the warmer air over the sea and creates a land breeze.

Land and sea breezes are most marked in a high pressure system with light winds. They can strengthen or reduce the prevailing wind or be completely masked by it.

The land breeze is not as strong as the sea breeze, but both usually do not exceed force 3. They can be felt for several miles on either side of the coastline.

## Forecasts

Apart from knowing what the immediate weather prospects are, it is important to be able to produce a chart showing the position of the weather systems and their possible movement. This not only helps to assess the likely weather in any particular area in which the boat is sailing, but it also shows what to expect in the adjacent areas through which she may later sail. In addition, it helps to determine probable wind shifts and strengths.

The information to produce such a chart, called a synoptic chart, is given in the BBC Shipping Forecast, which is broadcast four times daily (see below); other sources may also be used to fill in detail. See the end of this chapter for explanation of some of the terms used by forecasters.

As it is difficult to forecast exactly the speed and direction of approaching weather systems, it often happens that weather patterns change more quickly than expected, so that different weather is experienced from that forecast earlier. It is important, therefore, to listen to all available sources throughout the day and if possible to obtain a local forecast. Shipping forecasts are for a large area and cannot take into consideration the local differences so important to the small boat user.

### BBC SHIPPING FORECASTS

These are broadcast four times a day on 1500m (200 kHz) at 0033, 0555, 1355 and 1750 clock time. After the 0033 forecast there is a forecast for Inshore Waters (12 miles out to sea) which is worth listening to, as it may give an indication of local trends not obvious from the main shipping forecast, which covers a large area and does not take into account local

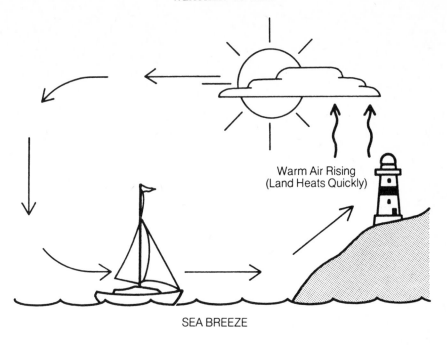

Warm Air Rising
(Land Heats Quickly)

SEA BREEZE

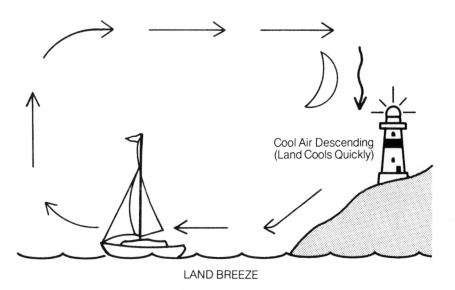

Cool Air Descending
(Land Cools Quickly)

LAND BREEZE

**Fig 9.6** A sea breeze by day is usually fresher than the land breeze at night, but neither often exceeds Force 3.

weather; the Inshore Waters forecast is also broadcast on Radio 3 (247m) at 0655.

### Shipping Forecast Format

The BBC Shipping Forecast follows a set pattern. It starts: 'Here is the shipping forecast issued by the Meterological Office at xxxx BST . . .' followed by any gale warnings in operation at the time. The general synopsis is given next, which consists of the position of the weather systems and their expected movement. After this, the sea area forecasts are given in the order in which they appear on the form. Final information is reports from coastal stations consisting of wind direction, wind force, weather, visibility, pressure and pressure change in that order. See example at the end of this chapter.

It is necessary to take down the information about all the coastal stations, even though they may be remote from your present position, as this, with the general synopsis, forms the basis of the synoptic chart.

### COAST RADIO STATIONS

Details of these will be found in the Admiralty *List of Radio Signals*, in Admiralty *Notices to Mariners* (Annual Summary), Admiralty *List of Radio Services for Small Craft*, and several nautical almanacs. These stations broadcast weather forecasts for their own areas, including any changes which may have occurred since the main shipping forecast; gale warnings are also included together with the synopsis. These broadcasts are in the VHF maritime frequency band.

### LOCAL RADIO STATIONS

Both BBC and independent local radio stations often repeat a portion of the shipping forecast covering their own area.

### LAND WEATHER FORECASTS

Radio forecasts for landsmen are useful, although they concentrate more on rain than wind; they often give a trend for a day or two ahead, and can provide background information to the shipping forecast. Details of timings will be found in *Radio Times*.

### TELEPHONE RECORDED FORECASTS

MARINECALL forecasts give information provided by the Meteorological Office for coastal areas around the British Isles for distances up to 12 miles off the coastline. They are updated two or three times daily. The information includes seastate and relevant high water times.

WEATHERCALL forecasts give a similar service but cover land areas. The correct time is included with both services.

TV AND NEWSPAPERS

These give weather charts, and sometimes satellite pictures, both of which are useful background information if studied a day or two before the intended passage and backed up with information from other sources. The *Times* and *Daily Telegraph* publish such weather charts.

LOCAL FORECASTS

Weather centres can be contacted by telephone for an individual forecast. Yachtsman's weekend forecasts are available for a small fee, with forecast charts for three days ahead for callers in person at London and Southampton Weather Centres.

It is often useful to talk to local fishermen, staff of yacht clubs, harbour masters, marina staff or anyone who uses a particular stretch of water frequently as they will be aware of any local peculiarities.

Local RAF and Naval Air Stations (ask for the duty forecaster) are usually most obliging.

COASTGUARD

The Coastguard broadcasts weather forecasts, from information supplied by the Meteorological Office, at regular intervals on VHF channel 67 (after initial announcement on channel 16). These broadcasts are usually at 4 hour intervals, but are 2 hourly when winds of force 6 or above are expected.

The Coastguard can also be called direct on VHF (channel 16 changing to channel 67) for a repetition of the most recent shipping forecast covering the local area.

FACSIMILE BROADCASTS

Equipment which was previously only suitable for larger boats has now been adapted for use by small boat owners. It produces an automatically printed synoptic chart but is rather expensive to buy.

SMALL CRAFT WARNINGS

These are issued by the Meteorological Office during the sailing season (April–October), when winds of Force 6 or more are expected up to 5 miles from shore any time in the ensuing 12 hours. They are broadcast by BBC and independent local radio stations, using plain language to indicate when the condition is expected, e.g. 'in the morning', 'after midday' etc. Broadcasts are made during the first programme break after reception, and repeated following the next news bulletin.

GALE WARNINGS

Gale warnings for all home waters are broadcast on 1500m (200 kHz) when winds of force 8 or above are expected. They remain in force until amended or cancelled, and are issued as soon as possible after receipt and then repeated after the next news bulletin. Coast Radio Stations also broadcast gale warnings.

The terms 'imminent', 'soon' and 'later' apply to a gale expected within 6 hours, between 6 and 12 hours, and after 12 hours respectively.

### Storm Cone

This is a visual warning of a gale, consisting of a cone one metre high with a base one metre wide. It is hoisted on flagstaffs at various places such as coastguard stations, port entrances and yacht clubs, whenever a gale warning has been issued. This has officially been discontinued in the British Isles although some yacht clubs and marinas still use it. In many areas the Coastguard broadcasts on VHF channel 67 (after initial announcement on channel 16) regular forecasts for inshore waters which include strong wind warnings.

For gales from any point north of the east-west line a north cone is hoisted apex upwards, and for any gale from a point south of this line a south cone is hoisted apex downwards. These are kept flying until dusk and then replaced (at some places) by lights forming a triangle, with the apex similarly up or down.

### SHORTHAND

In order to write down any forecast, it is necessary to use a form of shorthand because the detail is only given once, and often faster than can be written normally; it is also helpful if a prepared form is available such as the one illustrated on pages 94–5. The system used is not important, but it is useful if all members of the crew use the same, so that anybody referring to the form later will understand it. It is therefore a good idea to use standard abbreviations such as the Beaufort notation, an extract of which is shown below.

| | | | |
|---|---|---|---|
| d | = drizzle | G | = good visibility |
| f | = fog | M | = moderate visibility |
| g | = gale | P | = poor visibility |
| jp | = precipitation within sight | o | = slight |
| | | i | = intermittent |
| m | = mist | / | = after conditions in the last hour |
| q | = squalls | | |
| r | = rain | double | |
| s | = snow | letters | = continuous |
| w | = dew | capital letters | = intense |
| z | = dust haze | | |

Pressure tendency can be shown by lines as follows.

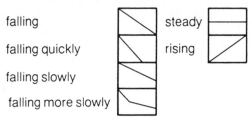

falling            steady

falling quickly      rising

falling slowly

falling more slowly

## The Synoptic Chart

The time for which the synoptic chart is plotted is the time of the coastal station reports.

Firstly, on the map (page 95) the reports from coastal stations are plotted, using abbreviations for the weather, filling in the pressure (using the last two figures of the millibar reading only, 1006 would be 06, 994 would be 94), and representing the wind by an arrow with feathers on the end, on the side nearest the low pressure; each full feather equals 2 wind forces (There is a compass rose marked with points on the form to help determine wind direction):

SW5

The information contained in the general synopsis regarding the centres of the systems is now plotted but, as the time of the synopsis is several hours prior to the coastal station reports, it is necessary to interpolate between their given position and their expected position 24 hours later, in order to produce a synoptic chart for the time of the reports from coastal stations.

Using the first part of the sea area forecast and ignoring any later changes, wind direction and force can now be plotted in all sea areas (if later forecasts are plotted, this tends to clutter up the map). Lastly all points of equal pressure are joined by lines to form isobars and the fronts are determined by looking for wind shifts and associated weather (see above, *Weather Indications*, page 81). The scale at the top of the map (see end of this chapter) shows the relationship between Beaufort force and spacing of isobars (at 2 millibar intervals), but this information is only approximate. There will not of course be an isobar passing through every coastal station, and usually much alteration is necessary before the final pattern emerges, therefore it is best to plot very lightly in pencil at first and perhaps join the stations showing equal pressure to get an idea of the shape of the system. The wind circulation usually shows the general direction of the isobars.

METEOROLOGICAL TERMS

*Anabatic Wind.* A wind blowing up a mountainside, caused by warm air rising.

*Backing.* An anti-clockwise change in wind direction.

*Col.* An area of intermediate pressure and variable winds between two adjacent highs and two adjacent lows.

*Forecast.* Details of the expected weather.

*Imminent.* Describes a situation which is expected within 6 hours.

*Isobar.* Lines on a weather chart joining points of equal pressure.

*Katabatic Wind.* A wind blowing down a mountainside caused by cool air descending.

*Later.* Describes a situation which is expected after 12 hours.

*Millibar.* A unit used to measure pressure on a barometer (barometers can also be scaled in inches).

*Movement of Systems.*

$$
\begin{aligned}
\text{Slowly} &= < \;\; 15 \text{ knots} \\
\text{Steadily} &= 15\text{--}25 \text{ knots} \\
\text{Rather quickly} &= 25\text{--}35 \text{ knots} \\
\text{Rapidly} &= 35\text{--}45 \text{ knots} \\
\text{Very rapidly} &= > \;\; 45 \text{ knots}
\end{aligned}
$$

*Precipitation.* Deposits of water to the ground, such as rain, hail, snow, frost and dew (not mist, fog or cloud).

*Pressure Changes.*

$$
\begin{aligned}
\text{Slowly} &= < \;\; 1 \cdot 5 \text{ mb within 3 hours} \\
\text{Quickly} &= 3 \cdot 5\text{--}6 \text{ mb within 3 hours} \\
\text{Very rapidly} &= > \;\; 6 \text{ mb within 3 hours}
\end{aligned}
$$

*Report.* Details of the existing weather.

*Ridge.* Usually an elongated portion of an anticyclone.

*Soon.* Describes a situation which is expected between 6–12 hours.

*Trough.* An elongated portion of a depression with V-shaped isobars (all fronts are troughs).

*Veering.* A clockwise change in wind direction.

*Visibility.*

$$
\begin{aligned}
\text{Very good} &= > \;\; 30 \text{ miles} \\
\text{Good} &= 5\text{--}30 \text{ miles} \\
\text{Moderate} &= 2\text{--}5 \text{ miles} \\
\text{Mist or haze} &= 1100\text{--}2200 \text{ yards (1000--2000 metres)}
\end{aligned}
$$

Fog = < 1100 yards (< 1000 metres)
Thick fog = < 400 yards (< 366 metres)

The shipping forecast uses the description 'poor', which is 2 miles or less.

BEAUFORT WIND SCALE

| Beaufort number (Force) | Mean wind speed (knots) |
|---|---|
| 0 | < 1 |
| 1 | 1–3 |
| 2 | 4–6 |
| 3 | 7–10 |
| 4 | 11–16 |
| 5 | 17–21 |
| 6 | 22–27 |
| 7 (near gale) | 28–33 |
| 8 (gale) | 34–40 |
| 9 (strong gale) | 41–47 |
| 10 (storm) | 48–55 |
| 11 (violent storm) | 56–63 |
| 12 (hurricane) | > 63 |

< = less than
> = more than

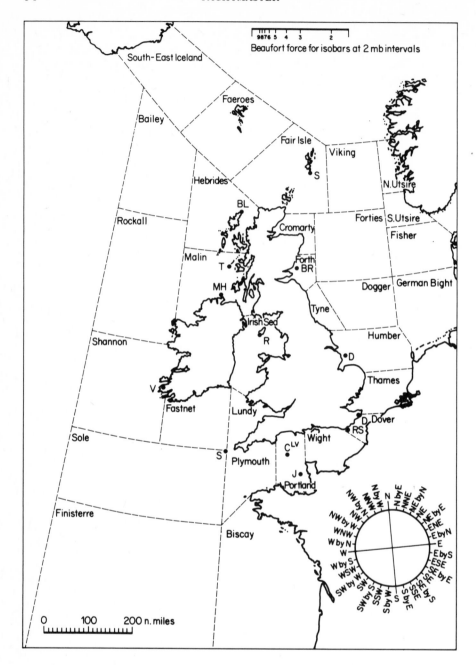

Beaufort force for isobars at 2 mb intervals

South-East Iceland

Faeroes

Bailey

Fair Isle

Viking

Hebrides

N.Utsire

BL

Cromarty

Forties  S.Utsire

Rockall

Fisher

Malin

Forth

T

BR

MH

Dogger  German Bight

Shannon

Tyne

Irish Sea

R

Humber

D

Thames

V

Fastnet

Lundy

D. Dover

RS

Sole

S

Wight

C  LV

Plymouth

J

Portland

Finisterre

Biscay

0      100      200 n. miles

| General Synopsis | Date | Time | | |
|---|---|---|---|---|
| Area Forecast | | Wind | Weather | Visibility |
| Viking | | | | |
| N. Utsire | | | | |
| S. Utsire | | | | |
| Forties | | | | |
| Cromarty | | | | |
| Forth | | | | |
| Tyne | | | | |
| Dogger | | | | |
| Fisher | | | | |
| German Bight | | | | |
| Humber | | | | |
| Thames | | | | |
| Dover | | | | |
| Wight | | | | |
| Portland | | | | |
| Plymouth | | | | |
| Biscay | | | | |
| Finisterre | | | | |
| Sole | | | | |
| Lundy | | | | |
| Fastnet | | | | |
| Irish Sea | | | | |
| Shannon | | | | |
| Rockall | | | | |
| Malin | | | | |
| Hebrides | | | | |
| Bailey | | | | |
| Fair Isle | | | | |
| Faeroes | | | | |
| SE Iceland | | | | |

Reports From Coastal Stations                    Time

| | Wind | | Weather | Visibility | Pressure | Trend |
|---|---|---|---|---|---|---|
| | Dir | Force | | | | |
| Tiree | | | | | | |
| Butt ot Lewis | | | | | | |
| Sumburgh | | | | | | |
| Bell Rock | | | | | | |
| Dowsing | | | | | | |
| Dover | | | | | | |
| Royal Sovereign | | | | | | |
| Channel L.V. | | | | | | |
| Scilly | | | | | | |
| Valentia | | | | | | |
| Ronaldsway | | | | | | |
| Malin Head | | | | | | |
| Jersey | | | | | | |

# QUESTION PAPER 9 – WEATHER TO SAIL

Answers on page 190

9.1   Plot a synoptic chart from the shipping forecast provided at the end of these questions, using the form on page 94.

9.2   At what time of year would the following be most likely to occur?
  (a) Radiation fog.
  (b) Advection fog.

9.3   List the cloud expected on the approach of a typical cold front.

9.4   A boat is making a passage towards the west, wind is SW. The boat is close hauled on the port tack. Approaching from the west is a line of heavy dark cumulonimbus cloud.
  (a) What is the likely change in the weather as this line of cloud passes over?
  (b) What action should the boat take?

9.5   There has been a lot of cirrus cloud in the sky, which has now been replaced by stratus cloud. The barometer is indicating a rapid fall in pressure. What type of weather may be on the way?

9.6   It has been a sunny windless morning, but towards midday a moderate onshore breeze springs up. What may have caused this?

9.7   The shipping forecast reported visibility as being poor. The coastline in the area covered by the report is 5 miles away, would it be visible?

9.8   Generally speaking, what might the following barometric trends indicate:
  (a) rapidly rising?
  (b) fairly high and steady?   (c) rapidly falling then remaining steady?

9.9   How are gale warnings promulgated?

9.10   In which portion of a depression would you expect the strongest winds?

EXAMPLE SHIPPING FORECAST (Synoptic chart page 191)

Broadcast at 1750

The shipping forecast issued by the Meteorological Office at 1700 BST:

There are warnings of gales in: *Viking, Cromarty, Hebrides, Bailey, Fair Isle, Faeroes.*

The general synopsis at 1200: Low North *Hebrides* 984 moving slowly north east and filling. Weak ridge *Finisterre.* New low forming west of *Finisterre* expected *Sole* by midday tomorrow. High Northern Spain stationary.

The area forecasts:

*Viking.* South or southeast veering southwest 6 to 8, rain then showers, moderate or poor becoming good.

*North Utsire, South Utsire.* South 5 or 6 veering southwest and increasing 7 later, rain, moderate or poor.

*Forties.* South or southwest veering west 6 or 7 decreasing 5 later, rain then showers, poor becoming good.

*Cromarty.* West 7 or 8 decreasing 5 or 6 later, showers dying out, good.

*Forth.* West veering northwest 7 decreasing 4 or 5 later, showers dying out, good.

*Tyne.* Southwest veering west 5 decreasing 4 later, drizzle then showers, poor becoming good.

*Dogger.* South or southwest 5, rain, poor.

*Fisher, German Bight.* Southwest veering west 4 or 5, rain, moderate becoming poor.

*Humber, Thames.* West or southwest 4 or 5, drizzle, poor.

*Dover, Wight, Portland.* West backing southwest 5 or 6, drizzle, poor.

*Plymouth.* Southwest 6 or 7, drizzle, poor.

*Biscay.* West 3 or 4, moderate.

*Finisterre.* Southwest 4 to 6 increasing 7 but cyclonic variable in the northwest, moderate.

*Sole.* Variable 2 or 3 becoming cyclonic, rain later, good becoming poor.

*Lundy.* Northwest veering northeast 5 or 6, showers, good becoming moderate.

*Fastnet.* Northwest 5 or 6 becoming variable 2 or 3 then southeast 5 or 6 later, rain later, good becoming poor.

*Irish Sea.* West veering northwest 5 or 6, good.

*Shannon.* Northwest veering northeast 5 or 6, good becoming moderate.

*Rockall, Malin.* Northwest 5 or 6 decreasing 4 later, good.

*Hebrides.* West 7 or 8 possibly severe gale 9 veering northwest and decreasing 4 later, good.

*Bailey.* Northwest 7 or 8 possibly severe gale 9 decreasing 4 or 5 later, good.

*Fair Isle.* West 7 or 8 possibly severe gale 9, but southeast 9 in north at first, rain then showers, good but poor in north at first.

*Faeroes.* North backing northwest 7 to severe gale 9 decreasing 7 later, rain at first, poor becoming good.

*Southeast Iceland.* North backing northwest 5 to 6 decreasing 4 later, good.


Reports from coastal stations at 1600:

*Tiree.* W 7, 18 miles, 1006 rising.

*Butt of Lewis.* W 6, 16 miles, 998 rising rapidly.

*Sumburgh,* SSE 9, rain, 2 miles, 994 falling rapidly.

*Bell Rock.* W by S 7, showers, 11 miles, 1006 rising.

*Dowsing.* W by S 5, drizzle, 2 miles, 1015 rising more slowly.

*Dover.* W 5, drizzle, 2 miles, 1020 rising more slowly.

*Royal Sovereign.* W 5, drizzle, 2 miles, 1021 rising more slowly.

*Channel Lightvessel.* W by S 6, drizzle, 2 miles, 1022 rising more slowly.

*Scilly.* WNW 5, showers, 11 miles, 1020 now rising.

*Valentia.* NW by W 6, 25 miles, 1018 rising.

*Ronaldsway.* W by S 5, 11 miles, 1012 rising.

*Malin Head.* W by S 5, 25 miles, 1009 rising.

*Jersey.* W 4, 5 miles, 1024 rising more slowly.

## Chapter Ten

# Anchoring, Mooring and Berthing

## Types of Anchor

There are various types of anchor, each with advantages and disadvantages. Some firms market their own special anchors, but the principles are similar to the types shown below. Typical parts of an anchor are shown in Figure 10.1(a).

### FISHERMAN

The traditional type of anchor is shown in Fig 10.1(a), and is sometimes called an Admiralty Pattern anchor.

*Advantages*
1. Can be stowed flat.
2. Good holding power in sand and mud.
3. Few moving parts to get fouled up or nip fingers.

*Disadvantages*
1. A heavier anchor needed than some other types to give equal holding power.
2. When stowed on deck, the flukes can do damage in heavy seas unless well secured.
3. Because there is a vertical fluke when it is on the seabed, there is a possibility of the anchor chain or warp fouling this, or the boat settling on it.

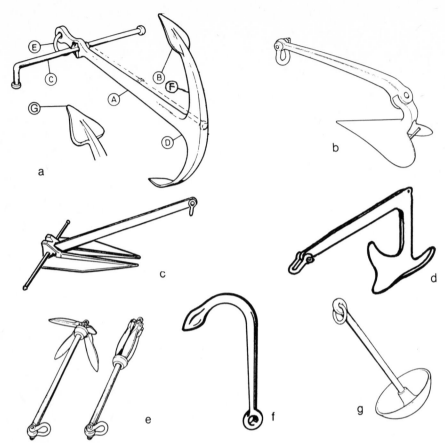

**Fig 10.1** (a) Fisherman anchor (b) CQR anchor (c) Danforth anchor (d) Bruce anchor (e) Grapnel anchor (folding type) (f) Rond anchor (g) Mushroom anchor. The parts of the Fisherman anchor are as follows: A shank, B fluke, C stock, D crown, E ring, F arm, G bill.

### CQR

The CQR is a proprietary type of anchor and shown in Fig 10.1(b). It is sometimes also called a plough. Imitations are often not as good.

*Advantages*
1. Holds well in soft sand and mud.
2. Lighter anchor required than a Fisherman to give equal holding power.
3. Usually digs in well unless the point impales a tin (filling the hollow portion with lead adds extra weight and encourages it to dig into the seabed).

*Disadvantages*
1. There may be stowage difficulties, and special chocks are needed to secure it unless fitted over the bow roller.
2. Movable parts can become fouled and damage the fingers.

3. Can capsize.
4. Can be difficult to break out of mud unless a tripping line is used.
5. Does not hold too well in kelp or hard sand.

DANFORTH

The Danforth is a flat twin fluke anchor with the stock built into the head;
Fig 10.1(c).

*Advantages*
1. Good holding power in sand and mud.
2. Less weight needed to equal holding power compared with a Fisherman,
   but about equal to a CQR.
3. Can be stowed flat.

*Disadvantages*
1. Movable parts can become fouled and can damage the fingers.
2. Not too good in rock.
3. Can be difficult to break out of mud unless a tripping line is used.

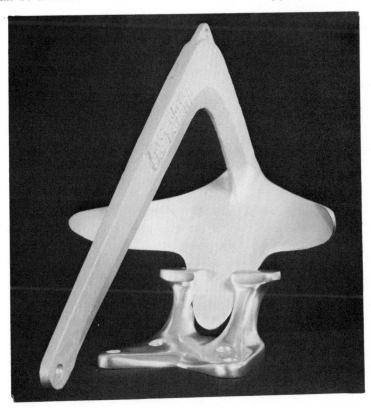

**Plate 5** A Bruce anchor from Bruce Anchors Ltd.

BRUCE

Shown in Fig 10.1(d).

*Advantages*
1. A much lighter anchor needed to equal the holding power of the other types.
2. No movable parts.
3. Digs well into the seabed however it lies, and quickly buries itself.
4. Good holding power in sand and mud.
5. Easy to break out.

*Disadvantages*
1. Difficult to stow without a special chock which, due to lack of space on the foredeck, cannot always be fitted. It can, however, be stowed over the bow roller if well secured.

GRAPNEL

A good anchor to hold on rock and useful to use as a kedge; Fig 10.1(e).

ROND

A one fluke anchor used for permanent mooring, so there is no second fluke left sticking up; Fig 10.1(f)

MUSHROOM

An anchor with good holding power used for moorings; Fig 10.1(g).

KEDGE

A small version of one of the anchors described above used for temporarily anchoring (when racing), for emergencies or for assisting the main anchor.

## Anchoring

Anchors hold best in mud, clay and sand; less well in hard sand, shingle or pebbles; and poorly in rock. Weed can clog movable parts with consequent loss of holding power. Where there is rock they can become fouled and, if the rock is covered with slippery weed, they can skitter across this without holding. The Fisherman is probably the best for holding in rock. Two main anchors, preferably of different types, should be carried, together with a small kedge.

Whichever type of anchor is used, if it is to hold without dragging, it must be subjected to a horizontal pull along the seabed, with plenty of

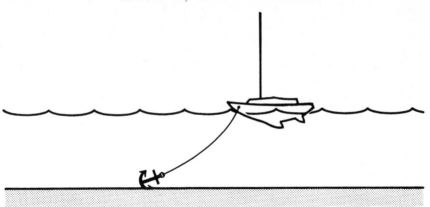

Incorrect—not enough warp or chain

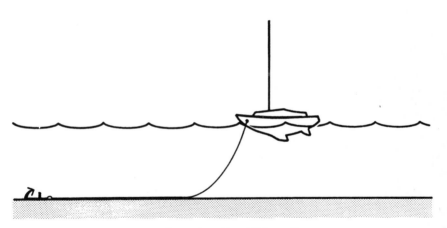

Correct—at least 3 times the
maximum depth for chain;
5 times for warp

**Fig 10.2** Incorrect *(top)* and correct *(bottom)* amounts of cable. If warp is used then at least 5 times the depth of water should be paid out. The pull on the anchor should be horizontal along the seabed to maximize the anchor's holding power.

chain or warp laid out; Fig 10.2. When breaking out the anchor this fact is used to advantage, because the anchor will not hold when the cable is pulled towards the vertical position.

For a larger boat, a full length anchor chain (ie 40m) is carried. For a smaller boat, a short length of chain (6m) and a nylon (elastic) warp can be used as an alternative. A comparison is as follows:

CHAIN

1. Heavy weight gives horizontal pull on anchor.
2. Weight of chain and catenary action complement the anchor and provide damping in rough seas.
3. The amount of chain let out (veered) should be at least 3 times the maximum depth of water.

CHAIN AND WARP

1. Length of chain (6m–10m) assists the horizontal pull on the anchor and reduces chafe.
2. Damping is achieved by the elasticity of the nylon warp.
3. The amount of chain and warp veered should be at least five times the maximum depth of water.

SCOPE

The scope or length of chain or warp veered will vary with conditions, type of anchor and size and type of boat but, if the anchor is dragging, more should be let out.

Whether chain or warp is used, both ends must be well secured. The inboard end should be fastened so that it can be quickly released. At the anchor, shackles should be moused to stop the pin turning. Warps, if used should be attached either with a fisherman's bend or with an eye spliced around a metal thimble, fastened with a moused shackle.

Before reaching the proposed anchorage, estimate the direction the boat will lie and the length of chain or warp required. This can be flaked down on deck, but this can sometimes cause accidents and damage to the deck. It should be marked at convenient intervals (5m) for depth identification. When the boat has reached the anchorage and has stopped making way through the water, the anchor is lowered and, as the boat falls back, the chain or warp is paid out. An anchor ball or, if at night, an anchor light (if the regulations require it), should be displayed high in the forward part of the boat.

The inboard end of the chain or warp should be secured around the samson post or foredeck cleat.

When the boat is steady, bearings of objects abeam should be taken, or a suitable transit noted, in order to check that the anchor is not dragging. The maximum swinging circle can be worked out to ensure that she does not swing into an obstruction when the tidal stream changes or if the wind shifts.

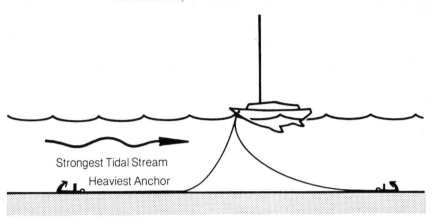

**Fig 10.3a** In calm conditions both anchors can be led out over the bow, the heaviest one laid towards the strongest tidal stream; but in a cross wind, both anchors may drag.

FOULED ANCHOR

If the bottom is covered with obstructions and there is no other anchorage available, the anchor is likely to become fouled. In these circumstances, a trip line should be fastened to the anchor so that it can be pulled up by the crown. There is a hole or ring on most anchors for the attachment of such a line. The other end of the line may be attached to a small buoy or led back to the boat and secured on board (a longer line is required if the latter method is used, but it avoids the danger of the buoy becoming a hazard to other boats). If the line is taken on board, care must be taken when raising and lowering the anchor to avoid a 'bird's nest'.

LAYING A SECOND ANCHOR

Sometimes it is necessary to lay a second anchor to reduce the swing or yaw of the boat due to tidal stream or strong wind, especially in a confined anchorage (the boat is then technically said to be moored). Unfortunately not all boats, because of their different hull configurations, lie at the same angle in identical conditions. Some will lie more to wind and some more to tidal stream.

One method of laying two anchors is to lead both from the bows, the heaviest one in the direction of the strongest tidal stream and the other in the opposite direction; Fig 10.3(a) This method is only suitable for a strong tidal stream with little or no wind. If there is a cross wind, both anchors will drag.

Another way is to position the two anchors well forward from the bows, with not too wide an angle between them. This method is used when

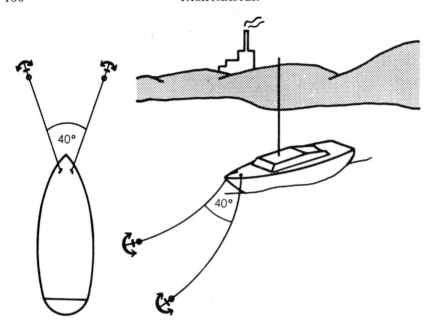

**Fig 10.3b** When strong winds are expected, and the boat will therefore be wind-rode and not tide-rode, both anchors can be laid from the bow, with about 40° of spread.

strong winds are expected and the boat will lie to the wind rather than to the tidal stream; Fig 10.3(b)

Anchoring fore and aft is not normally suitable for a small boat as it induces too much strain in a cross tide or a strong cross wind.

CHOOSING AN ANCHOR BERTH

The following points should be taken into account when choosing an anchor berth.

1. A place where the boat has sufficient chain or warp for the maximum expected depth.
2. Maximum shelter from all expected winds.
3. Clear of all obstructions as the boat swings.
4. Good holding ground free of obstructions on the seabed.
5. Enough water at LW to avoid going aground.
6. Out of areas used frequently by other boats.
7. With suitable transits or bearings to check whether the anchor is dragging, and to enable the boat to anchor in the chosen position.
8. If it is required to go ashore, near a suitable landing place.

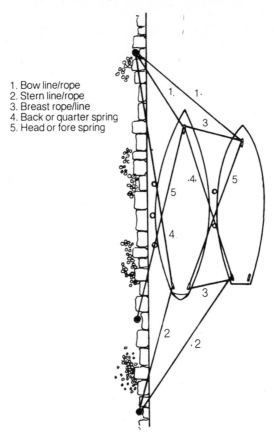

1. Bow line/rope
2. Stern line/rope
3. Breast rope/line
4. Back or quarter spring
5. Head or fore spring

**Fig 10.4** Mooring lines. Any line taken ashore must be adjusted as the tide rises or falls. Thus the outside boat must adjust her bow and stern lines, whilst her springs and breast ropes, which are taken to the inside boat, need not be adjusted.

## Berthing

Unless on a floating pontoon, when berthing alongside there must be sufficient rope to allow for the rise and fall of the tide; Fig 10.4. The ropes used for berthing will depend upon the size and type of the boat and the local conditions.

*Bow line.* A rope from the bows of the boat leading foward.

*Stern line.* A rope from the stern of the boat leading aft.

*Breast ropes.* Ropes abreast of the boat from the bows and the stern, these keep the boat into the berth; they should be slightly slack.

*Springs.* Diagonal ropes from the bows leading aft and from the stern leading forward, these stop the boat moving fore and aft and should be taut.

Points to remember when making fast alongside are:

1. If lying alongside another boat for more than half an hour, ropes from the bow and stern should be put directly ashore (many harbour authorities require this to be done). It is unwise to rely on the other boat's ropes especially if she is smaller, also if she wishes to leave before the outer boat she can then easily do so.
2. Adequate fenders must be placed between boats or between the boat and the pontoon.
3. Crosstrees should be staggered to avoid clashing in a swell.
4. When crossing another boat's deck this should be done across the bow section not across the cockpit, as quietly as possible, taking care not to tramp dirt or mud across it. It is courteous to seek permission first if the owner is aboard.
5. Rig frapping lines to prevent halyards slapping the mast.

# QUESTION PAPER 10 – ANCHORING, MOORING AND BERTHING

Answers on page 192

10.1   It is proposed to anchor overnight in a bay where the condition of the seabed is not known. The area is used by small power boats. What precautions would be necessary when anchoring?

10.2   Having anchored in the chosen position, how could a check be made as to whether the anchor was dragging?

10.3   It is proposed to anchor in a maximum depth of 8m. The wind is light with little tidal stream and the anchor has 6m of chain with plenty of warp. What is the minimum length of anchor warp to be veered?

10.4   List the important points when choosing an anchorage.

10.5   Which type of anchor is likely to hold best on rock?

## Chapter Eleven

# Buoyage, Pilotage and Lights

To assist safe navigation in coastal waters, a system of marks is used, called buoyage, usually consisting of buoys or posts. Some of these marks show the port and starboard side of channels, some indicate dangers, and some safe water.

The system of buoyage around the British Isles which has been developed by the International Association of Lighthouse Authorities, is called IALA System A and comprises three main types of buoy.

Besides being distinctively coloured, most buoys have topmarks and lights of varying characteristics. Nevertheless, topmarks are not always fitted to all buoys and this information will be found on an up-to-date chart or pilot. A full list of abbreviations will be found in chart number 5011 *Chart Symbols and Abbreviations*, which is in booklet form. See the front endpapers of this book for coloured diagram of IALA System A buoyage.

## Lateral Marks

These are used to show the port and starboard side of the channel when proceeding in the conventional direction of buoyage. On the port side of the channel they are red; if a buoy is used it is cylindrical (can). On the starboard side of the channel they are green; if a buoy is used it is conical (cone).

*Topmarks.* Port hand are cylindrical and starboard hand are conical.

*Lights.* Red for port hand, any rhythm: green for starboard hand, any rhythm.

### PREFERRED CHANNELS

At a point where the channel divides, when proceeding in the conventional direction of buoyage, a preferred channel may be indicated by modifying port and starboard lateral marks as follows:

*Preferred Channel to Starboard*
*Colour.* Red with one horizontal green band.

*Shape.* Cylindrical (can), pillar or spar.

*Topmark.* Single red cylinder.

*Light.* Red, rhythm composite group flashing (eg Fl (2+1) R).

*Preferred Channel to Port*
*Colour.* Green with one red horizontal band.

*Shape.* Conical, pillar or spar.

*Topmark.* Single green cone, point up.

*Light.* Green, rhythm composite group flashing (eg Fl (2+1) G).

## Cardinal Marks

These warn of a danger and are placed in relation to the four cardinal points of the compass, being named after the quadrant which they guard. They are pillar shaped buoys, and their most distinguishable characteristics are their twin topmarks and their black and yellow colouring; see diagram for details. The buoy always lies on the side of the danger indicated by the name of its quadrant. For example, a north cardinal mark would be to the north of the danger.

*Topmarks.* There are two triangular topmarks on every cardinal mark. A way of remembering how they are arranged is that north and south point away from the danger (when looked at on a conventional chart); west has the points together, like a Wineglass; east has the bases together like an Egg.

*Lights.* Light characteristics follow the clockface as regards the number of quick or very quick flashes: continuous for north (12 o'clock); 3 for east (3 o'clock); 6 plus one long for south (6 o'clock); 9 for west (9 o'clock).

## Individual Marks

### ISOLATED DANGER MARK

This marks a danger such as a wreck or a lone rock. It is placed over the danger, unlike cardinal marks which are placed around the danger. It is a pillar shape with black and red horizontal bands.

*Topmark.* Two black spheres.

*Light.* White, group flashing 2: Fl (2).

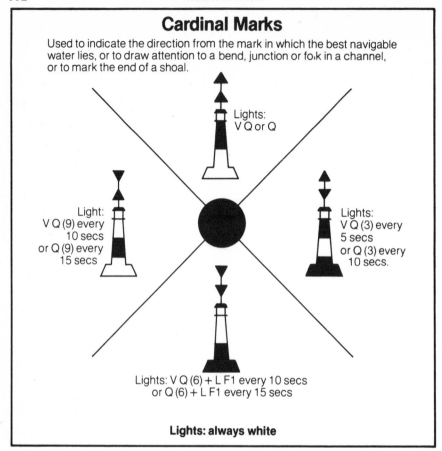

**Fig 10.5** Cardinal marks in diagrammatic form.

SAFE WATER MARK

This indicates navigable water all round the mark. It is spherical or pillar shaped, red and white vertical stripes. May mark the middle of a channel or may be used as a landfall mark.

*Topmark*. A single red sphere.

*Light*. White, isophase, occulting 1 long flash every 10 seconds or morse letter A.

SPECIAL MARKS

These are not navigational marks, but are of special significance, and the appropriate chart or pilot should be consulted to find out their individual meaning: outfall, practice area, water skiing etc. The shape is optional, colour yellow.

*Topmark.* A cross.

*Light.* Yellow, with a different rhythm from any white lights in the vicinity.


## Conventional Direction of Buoyage

Buoyage is laid in a clockwise direction around land masses, or in the general direction when approaching from seawards; Fig 11.1. If in doubt, the direction of buoyage is marked on the chart by an arrow.

When proceeding in the direction of buoyage, starboard hand marks are left on the starboard side of the boat and port hand marks on the port side.


## Pilotage

This is the art of navigating with the use of marks and other land features.

Larger boats are compelled to carry a qualified pilot for certain waters. There are also regulations for small boats entering some ports and, before entry to an unfamiliar place, a check should be made regarding any such regulations. This information is in the appropriate Pilot for the area, and any recent alterations will be published in the weekly copy of Admiralty *Notices To Mariners*; it is also found in various nautical almanacs.

It is a good idea to make a plan of a buoyed channel if it is unfamiliar, and to cross off the marks as they are passed; this way progress can be checked. In fog it may be necessary to work out beforehand the bearings and distance from one mark to the next.

It is not a wise plan to proceed along busy main shipping channels, but far better to stay on the shallow side of the main channel marks, still using them as a guide, as there is usually enough water for small boats to do this. This advice refers, of course, only to deep water channels used by merchant shipping.

Before entry to some ports, it will be necessary to know the state of the tide and the direction and strength of the tidal stream. There may not be enough water at the time or arrival, or it may be impossible to make progress against the tidal stream. If entry is not possible, an alternative plan should be ready.

Many ports have leading marks or lights which, when kept in line, guide the boat along the deep part of the channel, but in the absence of such marks suitable clearing bearings can be worked out. Careful study of the pilotage for the passage concerned is advisable, and for this a good yachtsman's pilot is useful, e.g. *Normandy Harbours and Anchorages*, *North Sea Harbours and Anchorages* and *North Brittany Pilot* to name but a few of the excellent series published by Adlard Coles Limited.

Always check on the port entrance signals, as some harbours will exhibit a light or shape if entry is prohibited; details are usually to be found in *Reed's Nautical Almanac* and in *Sailing Directions*. Some harbours such as Portsmouth forbid sailing yachts with engines from entering under sail.

**Fig 11.1** The conventional direction of buoyage in the British Isles follows the arrows shown.

# Lights

Details of all lights around the British Isles and north coasts of France are given in Admiralty *List of Lights and Fog Signals*, Volume A, and in various nautical almanacs. Information is also on the chart for the area, especially if it is large scale.

## RANGE

The distance over which a light can be seen is called its range. If all other factors are ignored and the earth is regarded as being flat, the maximum range at which a light could be seen would depend upon its intensity; this is called the *luminous range* of the light.

When visibility is defined by the meteorological office as being 10 sea miles, the equivalent range of a light is called *nominal range* (i.e. the luminous range for a visibility of 10 sea miles).

The curvature of the earth, however, has to be taken into account, as light travels in a straight line and anyone below the path of the ray of light will not see the light until well within the luminous range. When sailing away from or towards a light, a point is reached when the light appears to rise or dip on the horizon. This is called the rising or dipping distance of the light (*geographical range*). Obviously the higher the observer above sea level and the higher the light above sea level, the greater the distance the light will be visible, dependent of course upon its intensity; Fig 11.2.

There are sets of nautical tables which, if entered with the height of eye and the height of the light, will give the distance off when the light is rising or dipping; these are called 'Rising or Dipping Tables'. The distance can also be found by using another set of tables which calculate the distance

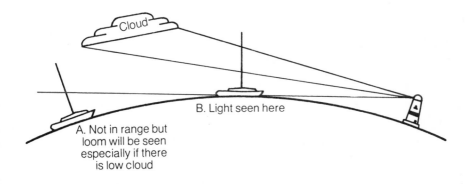

**Fig 11.2** The geographical range of a light at sea level is at B. However, vessel at A will be able to see the loom of the light reflected off the cloud.

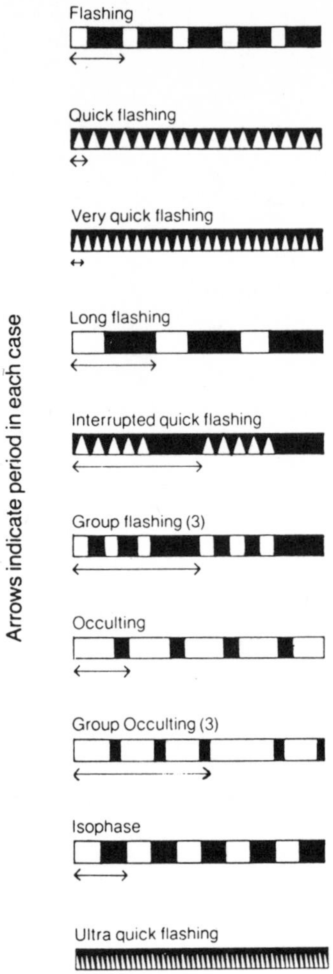

Flashing

Quick flashing

Very quick flashing

Long flashing

Interrupted quick flashing

Group flashing (3)

Occulting

Group Occulting (3)

Isophase

Ultra quick flashing

Arrows indicate period in each case

**Fig 11.3** The characters of lights in diagrammatic form. The period of the character is shown by the arrowed brackets.

from the horizon of the light, and the distance from the horizon of the observer which, when added together, give the dipping distance of the light. As the heights of lights are given above MHWS, an appropriate adjustment for sea level should be made for absolute accuracy, but this is not normally done unless the height of the light is relatively small compared with the range of the tide.

The ranges given on the charts may be geographical, nominal or luminous, dependent upon the age of the chart. On Admiralty charts after 1972 for Northern European waters, the range is nominal.

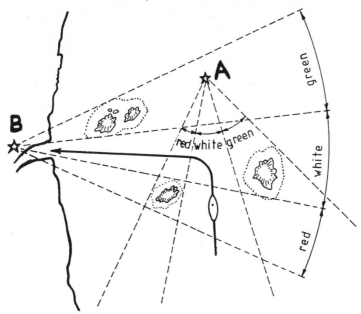

**Fig 11.4** Many lights have sectors of different colour: here the vessel must keep in the white sector of light A until she reaches the white sector of light B, when she can turn to port.

LIGHT CHARACTERISTICS

Lights have a timed period during which they exhibit their identification characteristics.

*Period*
This is the time in seconds that a light takes to exhibit its character plus any time it is eclipsed.

It is a good idea when trying to identify a light, to do so with a stopwatch and count the seconds. It is easy to make an expected light fit the one shown on the chart and thus make a wrong identification.

*Fixed (F)*. A light which is on all the time.

*Fixed and Flashing (F Fl)*. On all the time, but with a period of greater intensity during the flash.

*Occulting (Oc)*. The light period exceeds the dark period.

*Group Occulting (Oc)*. A number of occults within a certain time period: Oc (2).

*Isophase (Iso)*. The periods of light and dark are equal.

*Flashing (Fl)*. The dark period exceeds the light period.

*Group Flashing (Fl).* A number of flashes within a certain time period: Fl (3).

The number of flashes (or occults), is shown in brackets after the symbol, and this serves to differentiate on the chart from a simple flashing (or occulting), light. The abbreviation Gp Occ (2) or Gp Fl (3) may appear on some old unrevised charts.

*Long Flashing (L Fl).* With a flash of at least 2 seconds duration.

*Quick (Q).* The flash plus the dark period does not exceed 1 second.

*Interrupted Quick (IQ).* Dark between several quick flashes.

*Very Quick (VQ).* Flashing at a rate of about 120 per minute.

*Ultra Quick (UQ).* Flashing at a rate of 160 or more per minute.

*Morse Code (Mo (P) ).* Some lights flash a morse letter for identification, the morse letter being shown in brackets.

*Sectored.* Usually at a harbour entrance or on a headland. The light consists of coloured sectors showing green or white for safe entry zone, and red for danger.

*Alternating (Al).* These rotating lights have coloured portions. Each colour shows in turn as the light rotates.

# QUESTION PAPER 11 – LIGHTS AND BUOYAGE

Answers on page 192

11.1.   Describe the following light characters and give the international symbol used for each one on an Admiralty chart.
   The period of each is shown by the horizontal bracket:

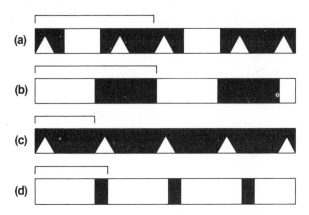

11.2.   A boat is approaching a buoy with the following characteristics: VQ (6) + L Fl 10s. What is the buoy and which side of it should the boat pass?

11.3.   What symbol (on an Admiralty chart) indicates the conventional direction of buoyage?

11.4.   When sailing in the direction of the conventional direction of buoyage, which side of the boat should the following buoys be:
   (a) starboard hand
   (b) port hand?

11.5.   A boat is approaching the following buoy from the north. Which side should she leave it?

*Chapter Twelve*

# Aids to Navigation

The principal aids to navigation, other than the compass, include:

1. Log (for distance and speed measurement).
2. Echo sounder.
3. Radio position-finding systems.
4. Radar.
5. VHF Radio.

It must be emphasised that these are aids to navigation and in no way replace the human eye and the compass. Electronic aids are becoming increasingly more sophisticated, particularly with regard to presentation of results and special gadgets. A simple instrument with a proven sensor usually gives the most satisfactory service, so be wary of equipment which is too elaborate.

**Plate 6** Excelsior towed log from Thomas Walker & Son Ltd.

120

# Logs

### TOWED LOGS

The rotating impeller towed astern on a plaited log line (plaited because it thus has no inherent twist in it, as does conventional laid line), driving a simple distance counter, has been used in different forms for over 100 years. Most of those made by Walker Marine Instruments have an accuracy of plus or minus one per cent and are essential for long distance cruising. The rotator has to be streamed at the beginning and hauled in at the end of a passage, which is sometimes inconvenient. The rotator can also be fouled by seaweed (but is easily cleared) and can, in appropriate parts of the world, be devoured by sharks. Some types have a speed indication as well, but speed is generally deduced by reading the log at regular intervals.

### ELECTROMAGNETIC LOGS

Modern electromagnetic logs use some variety of rotating impeller to send impulses to a display. The rotation of the impeller affects a magnetic field in the transducer, sending impulses to the instrument which converts them into a display of speed in knots and distance in nautical miles.

To be accurate, electromagnetic logs have to be set up and calibrated for every boat in which they are installed. They can be fouled by seaweed and may be difficult to clear. However, they are convenient and can be switched on and off like a light. Over long distances, particularly if the boat is pitching, their accuracy may not be greater than plus or minus six per cent. A towed electromagnetic log is on the market which may give improved accuracy.

Most electronic logs can be withdrawn for examination while underway; some incorporate a seacock to prevent taking aboard even a jugful of water in the process.

### DOPPLER LOGS

These logs have a detector inside the hull (i.e. no hull penetration), which measures ultrasonically the Doppler shift in the water passing within 3 cms of the hull. They require careful and accurate calibration and can overread by up to fifteen per cent, particularly in choppy conditions.

A different type of doppler log actually measures speed over the ground (in depths less than 130 metres) which is a considerable advantage.

### PRESSURE LOGS

These measure the difference between the static and impact pressure by means of a probe through the boat's hull, and are not normally used in small boats.

**Plate 7** The Seafarer echo sounder with depth alarm, from Seafarer Navigation International Ltd. This is a rotating dial type, and the transducer is shown below.

## Echo sounders

Electronic echo sounders, which are a most convenient substitute for the hand lead line, are among the most reliable and accurate aids to navigation to be found on most pleasure craft. Their transducers (transmitter/receivers) do not have to penetrate the hull and can be mounted either singly or in pairs to give high accuracy at all angles of heel. The transducers are mounted somewhere between the waterline and the bottom of the keel, so at low readings it is necessary to make an appropriate allowance for the depth below water of the transducer head. It is not a bad idea to go aground gently on one occasion and mark the depth scale at the precise point of grounding. In some echo sounders the scale can be electronically zeroed to correspond with the bottom of the keel. There are two basic types of echo sounder:

### ROTATING DIAL

The ultrasonic transmission is reflected off the seabed and displayed on a rotating dial by either a flashing neon or a light emitting diode (LED). This gives a clear reading, except in direct sunlight, though at night it is not possible to read the printed scale. It can also indicate the type of bottom (hard or soft) and at the same time intermediate indications such as a shoal of fish. If the depth is beyond the full scale reading, it can appear as a second trace echo. For example: full scale reading 30m, depth 35m, reading 5m. To check this, a range with a greater full scale reading should be selected.

POINTER

The pointer type of echo sounder shows only one depth indication, and the display, being a dial with a pointer, is much clearer to see and use without ambiguity. It is possible to have additional indicators or a digital readout.

## Radio Position-Finding Systems

Radio position-finding systems can be divided into four categories:

1. Radiobeacons with a non-directional transmitting antenna, of which the bearing can be determined using a receiver with a direction sensing antenna.
2. Directional radiobeacons in which the transmitted signal is varied between different bearings. Thus directional information can be obtained using a receiver without a direction sensing antenna.
3. Hyperbolic navigation systems which require two pairs of transmitters and a special receiver to measure the time difference between received signals. Some receivers will compute the boat's position directly, whilst others require special charts with an overlay of lattice overprinted on them.
4. Satellite navigation systems which work in conjunction with a network of navigation satellites orbiting the world to give regular and potentially very accurate position fixes.

MARINE RADIOBEACONS

Omnidirectional marine radio beacons are usually sited close to a lighthouse or lightvessel. A boat with a suitable direction sensing antenna can establish her position by crossing two or more radio bearings, which is particularly useful in restricted visibility. A small angular error at long range can considerably affect the accuracy of this position, so not too much reliance should be placed on a position obtained by crossing two radio bearings.

In coastal regions, radiobeacons are so numerous that a system of different radio frequencies and timings has been introduced to avoid interference. Groups of radiobeacons (up to six), transmit in succession on a set frequency, each for a period of one minute. This transmission consists of:

Morse identification letters (3–6 times) 22 sec.
Long dash for locating direction 25 sec.
Morse identification letters repeated (1–2 times) 8 sec.
Silence 5 sec.

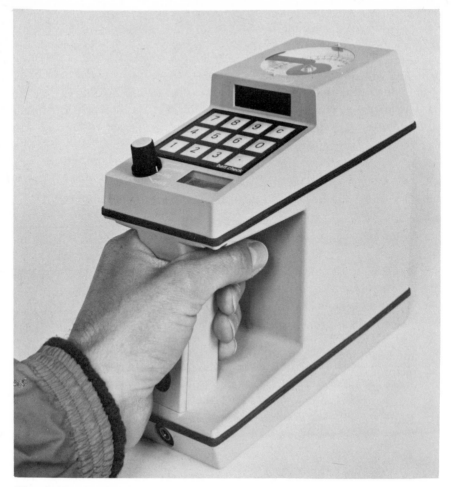

**Plate 8** The Aptel digital radio direction finder from APT Electronics Ltd.

The operating frequency, identification letters and timing sequence are found in either the *List of Radio Signals* or one of the nautical almanacs. The transmitting frequency range is from 285 kHz to 315 kHz.

On the chart a radiobeacon is shown as a small magenta circle with the letters RC beside it.

Radio direction finding (RDF) equipment includes a directional antenna, a receiver, a compass and some method of checking the received signal strength (headphones and/or meter). The antenna can either be a ferrite rod type or a loop type. When the axis of the loop is parallel to, or that of the rod is at right angles across, the signal path, the maximum signal is received. When the loop axis is at right angles, or that of the rod parallel, to the signal path, the minimum (null) signal is received. It is customary to use the null signal for directional information as it is more easily detectable. A compass (which gives magnetic bearings) is attached to the antenna to measure the direction of the antenna at the moment of the null reading.

Automatic direction finding radio receivers (ADF) either have an antenna which is rotated automatically, or which consists of crossed loops from which the directional information is obtained electronically.

The following sources of error have to be borne in mind when bearings from radio beacons are used for navigation:

1. *Night Effect.* The ionosphere, which is lower at night, can cause sky wave reflections which can distort incoming signals by several degrees. This effect is particularly noticeable one hour either side of sunrise or sunset.
2. *Quadrantal Error.* Incoming signals can be reflected by metal objects such as the mast or rigging. This distortion tends to be maximum when the signal is from a quadrant, for instance 45 degrees from either the bow or the stern. It is customary to break the electrical loop caused by the lifelines by introducing insulators or cord lashings.
3. *Coastal Refraction.* If the signal path from a radio beacon passes over high ground or crosses a coastline at angles less than 30 degrees, it can be refracted by up to 5 degrees.
4. *Ambiguity.* As two nulls can always be obtained with a two ended antenna, there is a possibility that the bearing measured may be a reciprocal. This is usually fairly self evident, though some RDF receivers do have a special sensing antenna.
5. *Homing-in.* When homing-in on a radiobeacon in restricted visibility, be aware that the receiver can give no indication of the distance off, so make due allowances for changes in depth and strong currents near the coastline.
6. *Compass Error.* RDF bearings suffer from all the errors to which the ordinary compass is prone.

It should be noted that some radiobeacons in foggy conditions phase their identification transmissions with fog signals; distance off can be determined by timing the difference in reception of the two signals (speed of radio waves versus the speed of sound).

AERO RADIOBEACONS

Aero radiobeacons are marked on the chart by a small magenta circle with the letters Aero RC. If they are close to the coast they can be most useful for navigation. They transmit continuously which is an advantage but, being normally sited away from the coast, they are subject to refraction errors. Transmitted frequency range from 250 kHz to 600 kHz.

RADIO LIGHTHOUSES

Radio lighthouses transmit on VHF at a frequency around 150 MHz. They have only a short range (20 to 30 miles), but are useful when approaching a port or estuary:

1. Tune VHF receiver to the frequency of the radio lighthouse.
2. Check identification signal.
3. Wait for the long dash.
4. Count the number of pips, which follow the long dash, until they momentarily cease and re-commence.
5. Refer this number to the reference lines on the chart to obtain a bearing of the radio lighthouse.

## Hyperbolic Navigation Systems

A hyperbolic system relies on ground transmitters whose accurate position is known. Two transmitters are used to obtain one Line of Position (LOP) and two others to obtain a second LOP. Where the two LOPs intersect is the boat's position. The two transmitters are synchronised and the times of arrival of the two transmissions are measured. If the boat is equidistant from the two transmitters, both transmissions will arrive together. If she is nearer one transmitter, then that transmission will arrive earlier. A measurement of the difference in time between the two received transmissions will therefore be a measurement of the relative distance of the two transmitters.

If all the points on the earth's surface where there is the same difference between the received transmissions were joined together by a line, then the shape of the line would be a hyperbola. The position of the boat is the point at which two such hyperbolae intersect. Normally an area is covered only by three transmitters: a Master and two Slaves. The Master transmits first and triggers the transmissions in the two Slaves. They transmit after the Master, but since their distance from the Master is known, the delay of these transmissions is known, and this is allowed for in the receiving equipment. Thus two LOPs are obtained, one between the Master and Slave A and the other between the Master and Slave B.

The hyperbolic LOPs can be shown on a chart but it is more usual for an on-board computer to work it out and present the navigator with his position in latitude and longitude. The computer also allows predetermined positions (waypoints) to be entered from which much useful navigational information (course to steer, distance to go, estimated time of arrival, speed made good, course made good) can be determined. Some systems have direct inputs of heading and boat's speed which enable the direction and rate of the tidal stream to be displayed.

DECCA NAVIGATOR

The Decca Navigator coverage in North West Europe is from the north of

Norway to the south of Spain including the Baltic, Sea. Other Decca chains are established in the Persian Gulf, Japan, South Africa, North East Canada, Nigeria, North West Australia, North West India and Bangladesh. The range limit is 300 miles from the transmitters. Within 50 miles of the transmitters an accuracy of 50 metres can be expected, but it can deteriorate considerably at night.

## LORAN C

Loran C coverage is the far North and North West Atlantic; the North Pacific and the Mediterranean. An accuracy of 200 metres can be expected out to the limiting range of 600 miles, but this decreases to 70 metres at closer distances. Loran C can make use of the transmissions reflected from the ionosphere (skywaves) which makes it less prone than Decca to deterioration of performance at night.

## OMEGA

Omega operates on a very low frequency (10.2 kHz) with a very long baseline (4000 to 6000 miles) between transmitters. This means it is essentially a world wide system. Accuracy varies from 1 mile in the North Atlantic to 6 miles in the more remote parts of the other oceans. Errors are at their maximum during night hours.

## CONSOL

A Consol transmitting station has a special directional antenna system (transmitting at a frequency between 180 kHz and 330 kHz), emitting a signal which can be picked up on any receiver tunable to the appropriate frequency. Because of the directional characteristics of the Consol signal, either a chart with a special overlay, or a set of special Consol tables (see *List of Radio Signals*, Volume V) needs to be used. The Consol signal consists of a station identification signal followed by a continuous note, then a 30 second keying cycle, consisting of 60 dots and/or dashes. By counting the numbers of the dots and dashes, the bearing of the Consol station can be obtained by comparison with the equidistant sector shown on the special chart. There are only two Consol stations operating in Northern Europe, one at Stavanger (Norway), and the other at Ploneis (France), so their convenience to navigators is strictly limited. Consol is a long range system.

## Satellite Navigation Systems

By using the navigation satellites orbiting the world, satellite navigation systems are capable of giving extremely accurate absolute (ie independent of any terrestial object) positions.

**Plate 9**  The SAT-NAV 801 Satellite Navigator with a remote reading speed indicator, from Thomas Walker & Son Ltd. A Sestrel bulkhead bracket mounting compass is shown sitting on top of the unit to give idea of the compact scale of this equipment.

Each receiver can pick up transmissions for about 10 to 15 minutes from each pass of an orbiting satellite. The satellite's exact position is relayed to the receiver, and from the transmitted signal the distance away of the satellite is determined. A micro-computer then calculates the boat's position, which may be to an accuracy of plus or minus 1 mile, though this depends very much on the accuracy of the boat's course and speed fed into the computer. As satellite navigation systems are developed, they will become cheap enough almost for universal acceptance by the cruising sailor who likes his navigation made simple.

### Radar

Radar is normally too large and cumbersome to be fitted on any but the larger pleasure boats. In operation it transmits a pulse which is reflected by objects in the signal path. Part of this reflected pulse is received by the radar and displayed as a pulse on a screen, which is either relative (with the transmitting station at the centre of the screen) or true motion. The distance measured by radar is very accurate, but the bearing can be up to 2 or 3 degrees in error. Detection and classification of radar echoes can be difficult in bad weather because small boats or buoys can be indistinguishable from wave tops, so it is advantageous if both the former two use radar reflectors to enhance their radar echo. Apart from detection of other approaching vessels, radar can also be used for coastal navigation.

## VHF Radio Telephone

Very High Frequency Radio Telephony (VHF R/T) is like a telephone with a vast party line. To avoid complete confusion it is necessary to impose a strictly disciplined calling and operating procedure. It is therefore a requirement that all potential operators should pass a test, and be awarded a Restricted Certificate of Competence in Radio Telephony (VHF only); or that they should be supervised by such a qualified operator. In emergency however, it is desirable that all crew members should be capable of initiating a distress call. It is also a requirement that a VHF R/T set is licensed for marine use, and that the installation in a vessel is licensed.

A VHF set operates at frequencies between 156·00 and 174·00 Megahertz (MHz). There are nominally 57 channels in this frequency band. The allocation of these channels is divided between Intership, Port Operations, Ship Movement and Public Correspondence (including radio telephone) with Channel 16 (156·8 MHz) being used for Distress, Safety and Calling. Operation can be either *Duplex*, in which separate antennae and frequencies are used for reception and transmission, or *Simplex*, in which a single frequency and antenna are used. Simplex requires a *press-to-speak* switch. The range of a VHF set is limited to line of sight, so the antenna should be mounted as high as possible. Another operating limitation is the 'captive' effect, in which a receiver will only hear the strongest transmissions, all other transmissions being completely excluded.

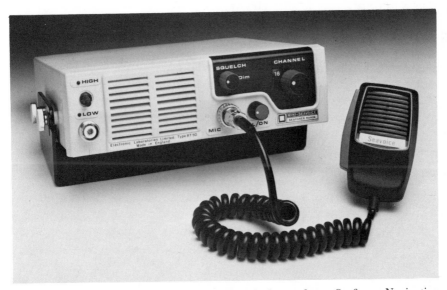

**Plate 10** The Mini-Seavoice VHF radio telephone from Seafarer Navigation International Ltd.

All this sounds most daunting to a potential operator, but with a little practice it becomes a simple routine and certainly opens up the capability to communicate.

The various operating procedures are now described. It cannot be emphasised enough that they must be followed and that transmissions on Channel 16 should be no more than are absolutely necessary:

## DISTRESS (MAYDAY)
(Serious and imminent danger requiring immediate assistance)

Select Channel 16 and switch on. Check that no other transmissions are taking place. Operate the press-to-speak switch (usually on the handset). Use the following *exact* broadcast procedure:

| | |
|---|---|
| 1. Distress call (3 times) | MAYDAY MAYDAY MAYDAY |
| 2. Callsign of boat (3 times) | THIS IS JETTO JETTO JETTO |
| 3. Distress call | MAYDAY |
| 4. Callsign of boat | JETTO |
| 5. Position | ONE FIVE ZERO BEACHY HEAD LIGHT ONE POINT FIVE MILES |
| 6. Nature of distress | STRUCK FLOATING OBJECT AND SINKING |
| 7. Assistance required | REQUIRE LIFEBOAT |
| 8. Other information | FOUR PERSONS ON BOARD |
| 9. End of message | OVER |

The sender may receive an immediate reply or acknowledgement from another ship, Coast Radio Station or Coastguard. If no reply is received, check that the radio is correctly switched on and tuned, then repeat the entire message at regular intervals. Once a reply is received and communication established, pass further information preceding each message with 'Mayday'. The position of the vessel is of vital importance. Do not give an apparently accurate position unless it is known to be so.

A vessel may initiate a distress call for another if the latter has no means of indicating her plight.

If a vessel receives a distress message she should listen for an acknowledgement by a Coast Radio Station or Coastguard. If this acknowledgement is not forthcoming and assistance can be rendered, then receipt should be acknowledged. If assistance cannot be rendered, then all steps must be taken to pass on the message to someone who can. The message must be preceded by the words 'Mayday Relay'.

## URGENCY (PAN PAN)
(Very urgent message concerning the safety of a vessel or the safety of a person).

Select Channel 16 and switch on. Check that no other transmissions are taking place. Operate the press-to-speak switch (usually on the handset).

Use the following *exact* broadcast procedure:

| | |
|---|---|
| 1. Urgency call (3 times) | PANPAN PANPAN PANPAN |
| 2. Address (up to 3 times) | HELLO ALL STATIONS |
| | HELLO ALL STATIONS |
| | HELLO ALL STATIONS |
| 3. Callsign of boat (up to 3 times) | THIS IS JETTO JETTO |
| 4. Position | TWO SEVEN ZERO NEEDLES LIGHT SIX MILES |
| 5. Nature of urgency | CREW MEMBER SUFFERED SEVERE INJURY |
| 6. Assistance required | HELICOPTER LIFT TO HOSPITAL |
| 7. End of message | OVER |

## SAFETY (SECURITÉ PRONOUNCED SAY-CURE-E-TAY)

(Important navigational or meteorological warnings).

Securité warnings are normally transmitted by a Coastal Radio Station. A call is made on Channel 16, but an alternative channel is used for the message itself:

SECURITE SECURITE SECURITE
HELLO ALL STATIONS HELLO ALL STATIONS
THIS IS NITON RADIO NITON RADIO
NAVIGATIONAL WARNING
CHANGE TO CHANNEL TWENTY EIGHT

on Channel 28:

SECURITE SECURITE SECURITE
ALL STATIONS ALL STATIONS
THIS IS NITON RADIO NITON RADIO
SHIPS ARE WARNED THAT DREDGING OPERATIONS
ARE DUE TO START IN SHIPPING CHANNEL EAST OF
NAB TOWER AT ONE SEVEN THREE ZERO HOURS FOR
A PERIOD OF SIX HOURS — OUT

## INTERSHIP AND PORT OPERATIONS WORKING

Initial contact can be made on Channel 16 but transfer must be made to a working channel as soon as possible. Intership operation is not for chatting or unnecessary messages. The transmitting boat should be identified on each transmission. An example of the procedure is as follows:

The initial call is made on Channel 16

YACHT JETTO
THIS IS YACHT MERMAIN
CHANNEL SEVEN TWO
OVER

YACHT MERMAIN
THIS IS YACHT JETTO
CHANNEL SEVEN TWO
OVER


On switching to Channel 72

JETTO
THIS IS MERMAIN
OVER

MERMAIN
THIS IS JETTO
OVER

THIS IS MERMAIN
PLEASE RENDEZVOUS AT HAMBLE SPIT BUOY
AT ONE NINE ZERO ZERO HOURS
OVER

THIS IS JETTO
MESSAGE RECEIVED
OUT


## SPECIAL CHANNELS

*Channel 6* is for intership search and rescue and, with Channel 16, is mandatory in multi-channel sets.

*Channel 67* is used in UK waters for exchange of safety information between HM Coastguard and small craft.

*Channel M (157·85 MHz)* is used by marinas and yacht clubs for control of safety boats, running regattas etc.

*Channel 70* is a reserved channel for use by automatic equipment in Safety Of Life At Sea (SOLAS) procedures.

*Channel 88* is used in certain areas for VHF Radio Lighthouse operations.

Public correspondence (radio telephone calls) can be made by direct contact with Coast Radio Stations, whose operating frequencies are shown in the Admiralty *List of Radio Signals*, Volume 1, and in some almanacs.


## Navigational Warnings – TELEX and FACSIMILE

For Northern European waters coast stations broadcast weather and navigational safety messages by teleprinter. The system is called NAVTEX. To obtain these messages a special receiver is required together with a miniature printer.

WEATHERFAX and OCEANFAX enable a ship to receive complete printouts of synoptic charts issued by national weather centres. A special receiver with a printing facility is required.


## QUESTION PAPER 12 – AIDS TO NAVIGATION

Answers on page 192

12.1   What is the best log to use for an offshore passage of 100 miles?

12.2   A rotating dial type echo sounder, using a scale with a full scale reading of 30m, shows a reading of 7m in a position where the depth of water is expected to be considerably greater. How can this reading be checked?

12.3   Radio bearings are taken of two stations both about 30 miles distant. The angle between the bearings is about 90°, but the accuracy of the bearings may be up to 2 degrees in error. What is the likely accuracy of the position plotted?

12.4   When and where are radio bearings most accurate?

12.5   Which VHF Channel should be used in an emergency?

*Chapter Thirteen*

# Safety

It is the skipper's responsibility to ensure the safety of the boat and her crew, not only by making the right decisions at the right time, but by seeing that all personal and boat safety requirements are complied with. The following personal requirements are a necessary minimum:

1. Plenty of warm clothes and a change of clothing.
2. Adequate wind and waterproof clothing, large enough to go over any other clothing likely to be worn.
3. Waterproof non-slip footwear.
4. Warm hat, gloves, socks and a towelling scarf (much heat is lost through the extremities).
5. Sharp knife with spike.
6. Lifejacket of an approved type, in good order.
7. Safety harness of an approved type, in good order, with two clips and a quick release fastening.

### Safety Harnesses and Lifejackets

In most cases it is better to reduce the possibility of falling overboard by fastening the safety harness line to a strong point on the boat but, in fog when there is a likelihood of a collision in which the boat might sink rapidly, it may be preferable to wear a lifejacket in place of the safety harness. Additionally, lifejackets should be worn by non-swimmers, and in the dinghy to travel between the boat and the shore, as this is where a number of drownings occur. The dinghy should *never* be overloaded.

Safety harnesses should be used in rough weather, (especially for foredeck work), at night or when alone at the helm. A sharp knife should always be carried (on a lanyard) to cut the safety line if necessary.

The lines on the safety harness should be too short to allow the wearer to fall in the water and be dragged along, as drowning or serious injury can occur if this happens, especially if the boat is travelling at a speed in excess of 8 knots.

With many designs of safety harness and lifejacket, it is possible to wear both at the same time and thus the choice as to which is better does not have to be made.

## Man Overboard

Sometimes, although all precautions have been taken, a person will fall overboard. An efficient method of recovery needs to be perfected both under sail and motor, which can be done by each member of the crew in all weather conditions. The preferred method will depend upon the conditions, the type of boat, the ability of the helmsman and the availability of other crew members.

Immediately a person falls overboard the following actions must be carried out:

1. The lifebuoy (and dan buoy) must be thrown in as near to the person as possible.
2. As this is being done *Man Overboard* is shouted loudly to alert all crew members.
3. If there are sufficient crew, a lookout is appointed immediately who points to the person in the water and continuously calls out his position. (In a rough sea or at night anyone in the water is quickly lost to sight).

The lifebuoy (and dan buoy) should have a powerful light for night use. Retro-reflective materials on all safety equipment and clothing are well worthwhile.

To help guide the helmsman to the pick up point, any buoyant object can be thrown in periodically to form a trail. If available immediately, a buoyant orange smoke cannister makes a good marker for day use, but as this is a distress signal it must only be used if the circumstances warrant. (Pains-Wessex Schermuly supply a buoysmoke for day use for marking the man overboard position. This gives off a dense cloud of orange smoke lasting for 15 minutes, and is combined with a night marker containing lights.)

If running with the spinnaker set, the course should be altered towards the wind and the spinnaker immediately lowered by pulling it down behind the mainsail into the cabin. A note should be kept of the time, course and log reading, in case the person in the water is lost to sight and the helmsman needs to retrace his course.

The decision as to whether to gybe, tack or start the engine to return for the pick-up depends upon the ability of the crew and the conditions.

Various methods are discussed below:

METHOD 1

Whatever point of sailing the boat is on, she immediately goes onto a reach (wind on the beam) and sails on for a sufficient distance to enable the boat to tack and return at a slow speed under full control. After tacking the boat reaches back, dropping slightly to leeward for the final approach which is made on a close reach with the sails flying so that the boat will stop with the person to leeward. (Occasionally if the boat is stopped head to wind, she will pay off on the other tack before the person can be secured).

Using this method the boat is always under full control, though it is necessary to travel some distance before tacking to give the boat room to manoeuvre and stop.

METHOD 2

As an alternative to tacking, the boat may be gybed round. If this is done too soon the person may be missed completely or, if the helmsman is inexperienced, an uncontrolled gybe can put the boat out of control and cause damage.

In light airs or when only a staysail is set this method may be used.

METHOD 3

Immediately heave-to and start the engine. The sails can then be lowered and the boat motored back.

This method is suitable with an inexperienced crew who might be unable to sail back, or at night when it is undesirable to travel out of sight of the person in the water.

If the engine is used, it is important to see that no trailing warps are in the vicinity of the propeller when the engine is put into gear, as this will immediately disable the boat and add further complications to an already serious situation. The engine must be turned off when the person is secured to the boat, as if it is left running in neutral it can be accidentally put into gear causing injury from the propeller.

METHOD 4 (MOTOR BOAT)

When this situation occurs from a motor boat or a sailing boat under engine only, the first thing to do is to steer the propeller away from the person in the water by altering course towards the side over which he fell. A tight circle is then turned to bring the boat alongside.

THE PICK-UP

*Preparation*
Whilst the boat is returning, two warps should be prepared: one tied to a floating object such as a quoit to use as a heaving line in case the helmsman misjudges the final approach; one secured to the boat to attach

to the person so that he is held whilst preparations are made to lift him out of the water.

The decision as to whether to bring the beam of the boat or the cockpit area alongside depends upon the method used for recovery. If singlehanded or using a tackle (attached to the end of the boom) to hoist the person out, it may be better to cut the guard rails and pull him into the cockpit. If the halyards are being used and there are plenty of crew to help, it may be preferable to bring him aboard alongside the shrouds.

As there are no halyards and sail winches on a motor boat there is an additional problem getting the person out, and therefore a ladder should always be fitted to this type of boat.

On initially coming up to the person in the water, it may be necessary for a crew member to lie along the side of the boat in order to reach him through the guard rails or, if the boat has a very high freeboard, there may be no alternative but to use the boat hook. Anyone attempting the pick-up must be securely fastened to the boat, as another man overboard will not help the situation.

If the man overboard is lost from sight or not immediately noticed to have gone over the side, the helmsman should sail a reciprocal course, and then start a search crossing and recrossing the suspected area where he was presumed lost.

The search and rescue authorities should be contacted immediately by any means possible.

RECOVERY

Anyone, even of small build, who has fallen in the water can become quite a heavy weight when waterlogged. The person is often shocked and cold and unable to get himself back on board, even with the use of a ladder or a loop of rope as a step. If it is necessary for anyone to go into the water to assist, he must be wearing a fully inflated lifejacket and be securely attached to the boat. Several suggested methods to help both a conscious and unconscious person to get back on board are as follows:

*Conscious*
1. A ladder: either a permanent fixture or a rope ladder securely fixed to the boat.
2. A rope or ropes with a bowline in the end in which to place the feet.
3. A rope with a large bowline in the end to put round the waist.
4. A sail halyard attached to the safety harness and the winch used to winch the person out.

*Unconscious*
1. A small sail such as the storm jib is hanked to the guard rail and a spare halyard fixed to the clew. The body is floated into the sail and winched

out. This method can also be used with a conscious person who is too
weak to help himself.

2. If it can be done quickly, it may be worth inflating the dinghy for use as
   a platform; should it be required, resuscitation can then be started
   immediately.

The best method to use can only be dictated by the circumstances. One
or more methods of recovery should be practised by everyone using the
boat, so that if anyone does fall in the remaining crew can handle the
situation without panic. Do not practise with a live person, but use a
weighted dummy (or a fender attached to a bucket). The action taken
must be quick, correct and efficient.

## General Safety

The amount and type of safety equipment carried depends upon the size
and type of boat and its cruising area. There are recommended lists in
RYA booklet G9 for craft under 13·7m (45ft). In the case of racing boats,
these may be subject to special rules.

Any boat of 13·7m and over must conform to the standards laid down in
the Merchant Shipping Rules; below this size the safety equipment is not
compulsory but strongly recommended. A general guide is given below:

1. Liferaft of a size suitable to carry all persons on board, approved and
   tested to date, carried on deck where one person can quickly launch it
   (most liferafts are launched in cases of collision and fire, not as one
   would suppose, through heavy weather).
2. A half inflated dinghy can be carried, but is a poor alternative to a
   liferaft and, in anything but sheltered inshore waters, is totally
   inadequate.
3. Lifebuoys, preferably two, one with a self-igniting light and a drogue,
   one with 30m of floating line attached ('U' shape is best, because this
   will fit under the arms of most people, whereas the ring type may not
   be large enough).
4. Adequate efficient navigation lights of approved installation.
5. Dan buoy with self-igniting light (useful to mark the man overboard,
   as lifebuoys will soon be lost to sight).
6. 2 strong buckets with lanyards.
7. 2 anchors of sufficient size with enough chain or warp for all expected
   depths and weather.
8. 1 fixed and 1 portable bilge pump.
9. An approved, up-to-date pack of flares with *at least* two rocket
   parachute type distress flares and a day signal. Make sure everyone
   knows where these are and how to fire them.
10. Radar reflector. There are several types available. In common use is
    the octahedral reflector which must be hoisted with the flat dish part

uppermost for maximum efficiency, (catch-rain position). Reflectors should be as large as possible and as high as possible.

11. A first aid box.
12. A waterproof torch.
13. Safety harness anchorages, one located near the hatch for use as the crew step into the cockpit.
14. A method of securing and releasing the hatch boards and cover from either side.
15. The name of the yacht displayed on the dodgers and on a piece of canvas to display on the coachroof if necessary; letters to be at least 22cm (9 ins) high.
16. A method of securing all equipment, such as batteries and any other heavy gear liable to do damage to the boat in heavy weather.
17. A radio receiver for weather reports.
18. A rescue quoit.
19. An efficient compass and a spare.
20. Sufficient up-to-date suitable charts and sailing directions.
21. Tow rope.
22. Tool kit which includes a hacksaw or bolt cutters.
23. It is desirable to be able to hand start the engine in case of battery failure, and a separate battery should be carried for lighting, isolated from the engine starting battery.
24. Some type of log to measure distance, and a lead line or echo sounder to ascertain depth.
25. RDF for passages out of sight of land, and a radio telephone desirable but not essential.
26. Strong and adequate guard rails and lifelines.
27. Fire fighting equipment: at least two 1·5 kg dry powder or equivalent fire extinguishers, fire blanket, bag of sand for oil fires.

## The Liferaft

The following instructions are for a Beaufort X type liferaft; they apply equally to most other types.

1. Make sure painter is secured to strong points.
2. Release slip knot and clear lashing straps from around liferaft container.
3. Manoeuvre liferaft to edge of deck.
4. Launch liferaft, standing clear of painter.
5. When liferaft is in the water continue pulling on the painter to operate the inflation of the liferaft.
6. Board the liferaft either by means of ladder or from the sea, do not jump on the liferaft (there may be someone inside already).
7. When liferaft is fully boarded, cut painter line with knife provided at the entrance.

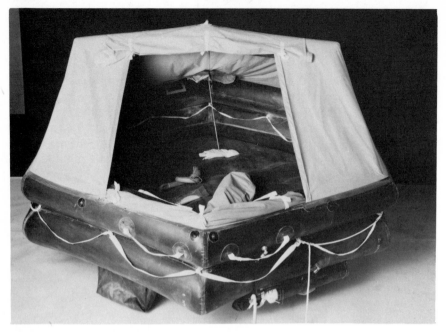

**Plate 11** A liferaft from Beaufort Air-Sea Equipment Ltd.

8. Paddle away from boat.
9. Look for survivors.
10. With the use of rescue line and quoit bring in survivors.
11. Stream drogue or sea anchor, when well clear of boat.
12. Elect a captain, usually the senior person aboard.
13. Check for leaks, and repair with leak stoppers if necessary.
14. Open survival pack.
15. Remove first aid kit, pyrotechnics and sea sick tablets.
16. Seal survival pack.
17. Attend to injured.
18. Pass around sea sickness tablets.
19. Post lookout with pyrotechnics, and form watch systems.
20. No rations of water to be issued for the first 24 hours unless to injured personnel losing blood. Do not drink sea water or urine. Keep warm.
21. Qualities for survival are in five parts, the last of which is the most important of all.
    1. Protection
    2. Location
    3. Water
    4. Food
    5. THE WILL TO SURVIVE

## Helicopter Rescue

Full details of helicopter rescue will be found in the Annual Summary of *Notices to Mariners*. Much of the information applies to large merchant vessels but the following points should be observed by small boat sailors:

1. The boat in distress may not be easily identified from above and should, therefore, be clearly marked with her name and sail number on a piece of canvas spread across the deck, or her identification shown in some other efficient way. An orange smoke is clearly visible from a helicopter.
2. If the helicopter is in the vicinity and the distressed boat thinks she is going to be missed, she should fire a red flare or an orange smoke.
3. A sailing boat should lower her sails and, as the helicopter cannot come low enough for the pick-up because of the boat's mast, survivors should be trailed well aft of the boat in the dinghy, or if no dinghy is available trailed on a long warp attached to the boat, wearing fully inflated lifejackets.
4. The boat's drift should be minimised by the use of a sea anchor.
5. Care must be taken when using smoke flares to ensure that the smoke does not get into the helicopter cockpit.
6. On no account must the winch wire be attached to the boat, nor should it be handled by the survivors as it can be charged with static electricity.
7. The instructions of the helicopter crew must be obeyed.

## Aircraft Search

Aircraft searching at night will fly a search pattern, during which they may fire green pyrotechnics at 5 to 10 minute intervals and watch for a replying red pyrotechnic.

## Fire

Much of the boat's interior is flammable and there is always a danger of fire from gas and engine fuel, especially petrol. Adequate precautions should always be taken to keep this risk to a minimum. Gas cylinders and spare fuel in the appropriate containers should be kept in a well ventilated outside locker which does not connect with the bilges. A regular check must be made for any leaks, and should any be found gas and fuel must be turned off at source, and any naked lights extinguished. The boat should then be well ventilated, particularly the bilges. Gas should always be turned off at the cylinder after use and the residue burned off from the pipes. There are various types of gas detectors available which can be useful.

The number and type of fire extinguishers to be carried depend upon the type and size of the boat. For the smaller boat, there should be at least two dry powder ones, one near the engine; a fire blanket should also be kept near the cooker to deal with fat fires (in an emergency a wet blanket can be used). A burning utensil should never be thrown over the side of the boat, as there is a possibility of spilling the contents and spreading the fire. Water must not be thrown on an oil fire, as this will spread it; sand or a fire blanket should be used. For non-oil fires a strong bucket with a lanyard is useful.

Foam extinguishers may also be used, so may BCF (bromo-chloro-difluoro-methane), but the latter gives off toxic fumes and must not be used in confined spaces. A notice to this effect should be placed on the extinguisher.

All extinguishers must be checked regularly for signs of corrosion. Powder type extinguishers can be shaken to see whether the powder is solid, and some types of extinguisher have a pressure gauge to indicate whether replacement is necessary, but in any case they must be serviced regularly.

Although it is not normally a good idea to launch the liferaft until it is needed (without anyone in it it is unstable and liable to turn upside down), in case of fire it may be necessary to do so to prevent it burning, especially if the boat is in danger of sinking. The inflated dinghy could also be towed astern.

### Flares

Pin point red hand flare is for use when within three miles of land or near other boats; it burns bright red for 1 minute. Red parachute rocket is for long range situations when a hand flare would not be seen below the horizon, it projects a very bright parachute flare to over 300m and burns for 40 seconds. Rockets turn into the wind, so aim vertically or 15° downwind if the wind is strong. Should there be low cloud the angle should be increased to 45° downwind, so that the rocket will be seen under the cloud base. Initially fire two flares with a one minute interval between.

*Orange Smoke Signal.* Hand held orange smoke signal produces a cloud of orange smoke for 40 seconds for use when within sight of help; for further offshore a buoyant orange smoke which burns for 3 minutes should be used. These show up very well from the air, but in strong winds may be dispersed blown along the sea surface and not easily distinguished from sea level.

*Recommended Packs.* No more than 3 miles offshore: 2 red hand flares and two hand held orange smoke signals. Between 3–7 miles offshore: 2 red parachute rockets, two red handflares, two hand held orange smoke signals. More than 7 miles offshore: 4 red parachute flares, four red hand held flares, two buoyant orange smoke signals.

*Care.* Stow flares in a dry place in a waterproof container where they are readily accessible, replace when expiry date is reached and dispose of the old ones by weighting and sinking in *deep* water. Should a flare fail to fire, keep in the firing position for at least thirty seconds and then remove the end caps and throw into the sea. See that everyone on board knows how to operate all pyrotechnics carried and follow the manufacturers' instructions.

## Flags

If flags are used they will not be distinguished up or downwind, and are only of use when within sight of help.

## Shapes

Again these are only of use if within sight of someone.

## Radio Telephony Distress Procedure

This is explained on page 129.

# QUESTION PAPER 13 – SAFETY

Answers on page 192

13.1    When should the following be worn:
(a) a safety harness
(b) a lifejacket.

13.2    If someone falls overboard, what are the immediate things the crew should do?

13.3    If in distress and a helicopter is in the area which does not seem to be aware of the boat's position, what action should be taken?

13.4    How should a cooker fire be dealt with?

13.5    What fire fighting equipment should a 30m boat with a cooker and an engine carry?

## Chapter Fourteen

# First Aid

It is important to be able to render first aid at sea, because it may be several hours, or a day or more if on a longer passage, before the patient can be treated ashore. Any treatment given must be quick, correct and thorough. It is essential to learn some effective form of resuscitation and to be able to treat hypothermia.

## Minor Ailments

Some common minor accidents which occur on a boat are dealt with here.

### CUTS

Unless deep or large, allow to bleed for a short while to help cleanse the wound, wash it clean with a little disinfectant, cover with a plaster. Cuts constantly exposed to seawater will not heal quickly.

### BURNS AND SCALDS

Immediately flood the area with cold water (fresh or salt) for at least 10 minutes and then cover with a clean smooth dry cloth.

### BRUISES

Apply a cold compress.

### SEASICKNESS

The only certain prevention is to stay ashore. There are some very good tablets which are quite effective in even severe cases, but these must be taken 2 hours before needed. It may help the patient to put him on the helm or give him something to occupy him above deck which requires concentration. In severe cases put the patient below lying down, and keep warm. Plenty of liquid should be given as constant loss of fluid quickly causes dehydration. Seasickness is aggravated by cold and hunger. If on deck, anyone likely to be seasick must be fastened to the boat with a safety harness to prevent falling in when leaning over the side.

### SUNBURN

Cover the affected part from further exposure. Cool the burn with calomine lotion.

### HEADACHE

Sometimes caused by glare. Aspirin and sunglasses may help.

### STRAINS AND SPRAINS

Rest the limb in the most comfortable position.

## Major Accidents

The most that can be done is to prevent major accidents from getting any worse and to make the patient as comfortable as possible.

### DISLOCATIONS, FRACTURES

Immobilise in the most comfortable position and get the patient ashore for hospitalisation as quickly as possible.

### SEVERE BLEEDING

This must be stopped, by pinching the flesh together, raising the limb or applying pads of material pressed onto the wound. Do not apply a tourniquet. Pressure points are only to be used in emergency unless you are skilled.

### INTERNAL BLEEDING

Lie the patient down, keep warm and quiet, get quickly ashore for hospitalisation.

### SHOCK

This accompanies most injuries and can kill if not treated. The symptoms are pallor, clammy skin, profuse sweating, vomiting, thirst, anxiety, pulse weak or thready, and shallow or rapid breathing. The treatment is to lie the casualty down and treat the underlying injury. Keep the head low and turned to one side in case of vomiting, so that the person will not choke, loosen clothing, and do not apply heat but warm up with a blanket and reassure.

### CONCUSSION COMPRESSION

This can occur after a blow on the head. The patient may go into a coma or become drowsy. If there is a bone penetrating the brain or fluid collecting around it, the brain can become compressed and unconsciousness occur, when breathing may cease and death result. All bumps on the head should be regarded as serious and the patient watched. If in any doubt, the patient should be referred to hospital, as unconsciousness can occur several hours later.

Immediate treatment is to loosen clothing, watch breathing, dress any wounds and place the patient on the side with the head low and turned to the side in case vomiting occurs. Treat for shock.

## Resuscitation

When breathing has stopped, quick action is necessary to restart it and some method of resuscitation must be applied. Even after only a few minutes the brain can be damaged if starved of oxygen. Every member of a boat's crew should be proficient in administering some efficient method of resuscitation. The main points of expired air resuscitation (EAR) are set out below, but this is only a guide and it should be learned under expert supervision, using a mannequin.

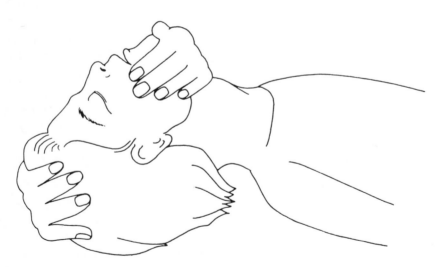

**Fig 14.1** The correct position of the head for mouth-to-mouth resuscitation.

1. Lie the patient on his back.
2. Kneeling by his shoulder, clear the mouth of any obvious obstructions, check to see whether he has swallowed his tongue but do not waste time.
3. Put one hand under the patient's neck and the other on his forehead.
4. Gently lift under the neck with one hand and push the forehead back with the other, whilst pinching the nose with the thumb and forefinger; this is to create an open airway.
5. Seal your mouth around the patient's and give several quick breaths, still pinching the nose with the thumb and forefinger to stop air escaping.
6. Take a deep breath, seal your mouth around the patient's again and blow. The chest should be seen to rise.
7. Remove your mouth from the patient's and let the air escape naturally from his lungs, then repeat the process blowing into the patient's mouth about 12–14 times a minute; make sure a good seal is made with your mouth.
8. Continue until there is no chance of recovery or until the patient recovers his own ability to breath.
9. If normal breathing is established, the patient must be carefully watched to see that his breathing does not fail again.

A rough guide as to how many breaths per minute to administer for an adult, is to your own natural breathing rhythm. For small children and babies more breaths are needed, but care must be taken not to blow too hard or lung damage will occur.

If the chest is not seen to rise, a good seal is probably not being made, or there is an obstruction, also the tilt of the head to ensure a good airway should be checked.

Should the heart have stopped, closed chest cardiac massage can be applied, but unless this has been properly learned and is correctly administered, it will not be effective and damage can result. It should never be practised on a person whose heart is still beating.

Any person who has been apparently drowned must be treated in hospital as soon as possible because, even thought they appear to have recovered, they may die hours later.

## Hypothermia

This is a severe cooling of the inner core of the body from which death can result, caused by continued exposure to a cold environment, such as being in the sea, or even on the boat, if inadequately clothed.

SYMPTOMS

Collapse, complaining of the cold or shivering in the early stages, cramp, irritability, unnatural quietness, lack of co-ordination, loss of energy, forgetfulness, pallor and cold to the touch.

TREATMENT

In dealing with a patient suffering from hypothermia in a boat at sea, it is often a question of what is the most suitable treatment with the facilities available.

If the patient has been in the water, on rescue a check should be made to see whether he is still breathing. If not the airway should be checked to see if it is clear and expired air resuscitation started immediately.

He should be insulated to prevent further heat loss, and an attempt made to seek assistance by radio or any means available. If breathing is satisfactory but the patient is cold, rigid or shivering, place in a sleeping bag or wrap in blankets and lay on a bunk with the legs slightly elevated.

He should be constantly observed to see that the airway is kept clear and that his condition does not deteriorate.

Unless expert medical advice is at hand, rewarming should be slow (not with hot water bottles etc). A very cold patient may shiver for many hours, before the heat generated and retained inside the insulating layers of blankets or sleeping bags will eventually rewarm the body.

A conscious patient may be given hot sweet drinks on demand during the rewarming process, but not alcoholic stimulants as these only serve to give an impression of warmth and cause the blood to go to the surface, so that body heat is lost more rapidly.

When lifted from the water, the patient should be handled gently and kept in the horizontal position.

## Recovery or Coma Position

If a patient is unconscious or vomiting is likely to occur (provided there is no injury to prevent it), he should be placed in the recovery or coma position, with the lower arm and leg straight and the upper arm and leg bent. The head should be turned sideways and a pad such as a pillow or

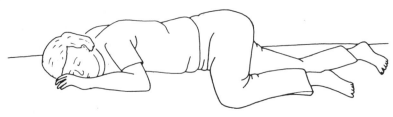

**Fig 14.2** The recovery or coma position.

coat placed under the chest to prevent him rolling over. In this position a clear airway is maintained, the patient will not choke if he vomits and the tongue cannot fall backwards and block the throat.

## Contents Of A First Aid Kit

Keep the first aid kit in a watertight box and list the contents on the outside of the box. This is a basic list:

Roll of Plaster
Individual plasters
Large triangular bandages
Small bandages
Lint
Cotton wool
Scissors
Tweezers
Eye lotion and eye bath
Calomine lotion
Safety pins
Disinfectant
Aspirin
Seasickness tablets
Indigestion tablets
Exposure bag
First aid book

For long distances, some doctors will make up a kit containing anti-biotics, anaesthetics and other items which normally need a prescription.

# QUESTION PAPER 14 – FIRST AID

Answers on page 193

14.1   Someone has burned their arm badly on an outboard motor, what is the first thing to do?

14.2   A member of the crew is being continually seasick and not responding to any treatment. It is a rough day and the boat cannot reach port for at least 6 hours. What action should be taken?

14.3   Several hours after receiving a severe hit on the head with the boom the patient is becoming drowsy. What would you suspect from this condition?

14.4   What treatment should be administered to a person who has been found unconscious floating in an inflated lifejacket?

14.5   Shock accompanies most injuries, what can be done to alleviate this?

*Chapter Fifteen*

# Fog and Heavy Weather

## Fog

If fog is seen to be approaching, immediate action should be to obtain a fix of position. If this is not possible the best known position should be worked out from the last available information. A written record of positions and courses (called a deck or boat log) should always be regularly kept. If this has not been done and no fix is available any further action is unreliable.

In dense fog when the coastline cannot be seen and normal bearings are not possible, two immediate dangers occur:

1. Being run down by a larger boat which will probably be unaware of a small boat's presence (radar on big ships does not always pick up the echo from a small boat).
2. Going aground.

All available instruments which will help to fix the boat's position should be used. For example, the echo sounder should be started if a line of soundings is possible or there is a danger of going aground.

It is important to keep a steady course and speed, as constant changes make accurate navigation difficult or impossible; the speed should be slow enough to stop or alter course at the first signs of danger.

Great care must be taken if another vessel is heard close at hand, and the following precautions should be taken to ensure the safety of the crew and the boat:

1. Inflated lifejackets must be worn; these can save lives in case of collision.
2. A good lookout should be posted in the bows to report to the helmsman everything, however trivial, observed or heard, and a good listening watch should be maintained by every crew member for the fog signals of other boats or navigational marks. If in doubt, course should be altered away from the suspected danger.
3. The appropriate fog signal should be sounded.
4. Silence must be maintained by all the crew.

5. The radar reflector should be hoisted as high as possible.
6. All safety equipment must be checked over and made ready for immediate use. If a liferaft is not carried the dinghy should be fully inflated and towed astern.
7. The anchor should be ready to let go quickly.
8. Flares, especially white ones, should be easily to hand.
9. If the engine is not already in use it should be turned over so that it is ready if needed.
10. If the engine is being used it may be turned off periodically to listen, but if this is done a careful check of how far the boat drifts in the time the engine is off must be kept.

WHERE TO BE

The decision as to whether to carry on towards the intended destination, or alter course away from it will depend upon the original destination, where the boat was at the time the fog closed in (and the accuracy of the latest fix), the instruments available, and the ability and experience of the navigator. There are several courses of action:

1. Go inshore at right angles to the coast, using the echo sounder, and try to pick up a contour line so that a course parallel to the shore can be maintained. The advantage of this action is that it keeps the boat in shallower water not used by larger boats, and so the chances of collision are minimised. Accurate and careful navigation is needed to avoid grounding and inshore hazards. It may, however, be possible to see the coast close inshore and use the headlands for fixes.
2. If a safe anchorage can be found, the boat can anchor and hope the fog will lift. This is a wise thing to do when approaching a port entrance as, unless it is well known or has a comparatively easy entry, it is much safer to wait for the fog to lift.
3. Standing offshore in deeper water may be better on an outward passage or if there are a lot of inshore hazards but, as larger boats also use the deeper water, a constant and careful lookout is even more important. On no account stay in the shipping lanes. If caught in a shipping lane, leave it as quickly as possible.

AIDS TO NAVIGATION IN FOG

The compass is of prime importance, as without it direction cannot be determined in a fog and accurate navigation is impossible. A reliable log to record distance is necessary and an echo sounder or lead line to ascertain depth. A radio direction finder is very useful and may mean safe continuation of an otherwise difficult and hazardous journey. Radar makes fog navigation a lot easier, but it is expensive and quite large for a small boat to carry. It does give a picture of *everything* all round the boat, but experience in interpretation is necessary.

Radiobeacons which broadcast a synchronised sound signal can be used if they are in the vicinity.

It is always important to write up the boat's log at regular intervals, showing all available information. In fog this is extremely necessary so that an EP can be worked out when required. In case of collision or accident, this record may be needed by the insurance company or the Department of Trade.

If weather reports have been regularly checked and a forecast obtained from the local weather office, the boat can often avoid setting out when a risk of fog exists, but sooner or later, however many precautions are taken, the boat will be caught out in a dense fog and all possible actions for safety must be taken.

## Heavy Weather

If shipping forecasts have been studied and weather reports obtained regularly, there will usually be some warning of approaching bad weather.

If still in port and there is any doubt as to the ability of the crew, the seaworthiness of the boat or the severity of the threatening weather, the boat should not leave. Had this decision been made on some occasions, the coastguard would not have had to go out searching for survivors.

If at sea and there is no suitable port near at hand which can be safely entered in the worst expected conditions, preparations must be made to ensure the safety of the crew and the boat.

### SAILS

Sails should be reefed or changed down in good time. Being overcanvassed when a severe storm hits the boat is the cause of much of the trouble encountered by the unwise sailor. It is too late and too dangerous to reef after the event, but should this have to be done, the minimum number of crew should be on the foredeck, and their safety harness clips should be securely fastened to a strong point.

A trysail, which is a small strong, loose footed sail, can be used instead of the mainsail. This saves wear on the mainsail and enables the main boom to be lashed down, but it may take some time to fit unless there is a special track on the mast, also the boat cannot sail as close to the wind as with a deeply reefed mainsail. Some long distance sailors keep such a sail permanently fitted on its own track ready to hoist quickly when needed.

STOWAGE

All gear must be stowed securely both above and below deck. Much damage can be done by heavy objects hitting the hull of the boat. See that all safety equipment is accessible and ready for immediate use.

Turn the engine over to check that it will start if needed.

If there is time, prepare food and hot soup in a vacuum flask, as this will be appreciated later when there is not much chance of anyone going below if conditions are severe. One of the contributory factors to seasickness is becoming cold through lack of food; hypothermia is then a risk.

Everyone must wear an efficient safety harness, which *must* be clipped on to a strong point if there is any danger of falling overboard. It is wise to clip on when leaving the cabin before climbing up on to the deck, as at this point most people are balanced on one foot and are unstable. Guardrails are *not* strongpoints.

Washboards and hatch covers must be in position and fixed so that they cannot accidentally come undone, and if there are storm boards, these should be put in place.


BOAT HANDLING IN HEAVY WEATHER

*Trailing Warps*
Sometimes it is better to run before the wind with only a small amount of sail area if there is plenty of sea room, trailing long heavy warps behind to keep the boat steady. Shallow water causes otherwise fairly regular seas to become confused due to upsurge from the bottom, with consequent danger of a rogue cross-wave; this effect starts at about 10 fathoms or 20m. Often the boat will be safer offshore, especially if there is a danger of being blown onto a leeshore.


*Lying A-hull*
Some boats will lie quite well with no sails hoisted at all with the tiller to leeward (lying a-hull), however as the broadside of the boat will be presented to the weather she will roll badly. Many modern sailing boats lie with the bows away from the wind, and much damage can then be caused by breaking waves.


*Heaving-to*
If the boat can heave-to comfortably, and there is plenty of searoom, this can give breathing space to cope with an emergency, to reef, or to go below for a quick meal.

The easiest way to heave-to is to tack, leaving the foresail cleated; when the foresail backs, the helm is brought to leeward and secured. The mainsail is adjusted according to the size of the foresail. This is thus an easy manoeuvre which results in a boat nearly stationary, with the foresail

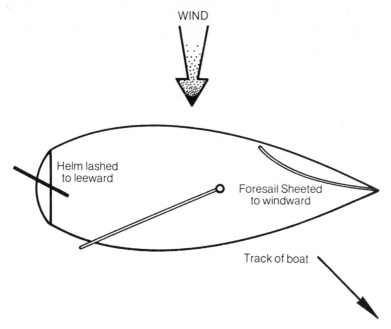

WIND

Helm lashed
to leeward

Foresail Sheeted
to windward

Track of boat

**Fig 15.1** Heaving-to. The helm is lashed to leeward and the foresail sheeted to windward. The drive of the mainsail is thus counteracted, and the boat should lie comfortably riding the seas making slow forward leeway.

backed counteracting the forward drive of the mainsail. The boat's motion is steady and gives the opportunity in rough weather of a break for a rest; Fig 15.1.

When hove-to the boat will make considerable leeway, but she can be tacked if there is a navigational hazard to leeward.

### Motorboats

If the boat is a motorboat, it has to conserve fuel and attempt to gain a suitable port or shelter before this is exhausted. It may be necessary to motor gently into the weather to keep the bows into breaking waves.

### LEESHORE

In rough weather there is always the danger of a leeshore, one on to which the wind is blowing and the seas breaking. Particularly dangerous is a gradually shelving beach between two headlands. In strong winds a boat should keep well clear.

Frequently what appears to be a safe harbour requires an approach close to a leeshore. The prudence of such an approach must be carefully considered as it may well be safer to choose an alternative harbour, to remain at sea or to wait for high tide when the seas may be flatter. In the event of engine failure it can be difficult to get away from a leeshore, as it is quite likely that even the heaviest anchor, with all available chain let out, may drag in the heavy swell.

# QUESTION PAPER 15 – FOG AND HEAVY WEATHER

Answers on page 193

15.1   What is the first thing to do when visibility is rapidly deteriorating, and what further precautions should be taken?

15.2   A boat is on a 24 hour passage, the wind is W 3–4, her course is southerly. The following weather report is received for the local sea area, 'gale force 8 imminent'. What precautions should be taken for the safety of the boat and the safety and comfort of the crew?

15.3   A boat is motoring in thick fog when somewhere ahead a prolonged blast every two minutes is heard. What should be done?

15.4   A sudden gale overtakes a boat which is then greatly overcanvassed. It is obviously necessary to reef down a lot of the mainsail, which is of the roller reefing type but very rough for deckwork. How could this be done safely minimising the boat's movement?

15.5   What are the advantages and disadvantages of a trysail compared with a deeply reefed mainsail?

*Chapter Sixteen*

# Collision Rules

It is absolutely necessary to have a sound knowledge of all collision rules, and this chapter should be read in conjunction with a copy of International Regulations for Preventing Collisions At Sea.
*Note*: Extracts of the Convention on the International Regulations for Preventing Collisions at Sea, 1972, reprinted by permission of IMO.

RULE 5 LOOK-OUT

*Every vessel shall at all times maintain a proper look-out by sight and hearing as well as by all available means appropriate in the prevailing circumstances and conditions so as to make a full appraisal of the situation and of the risk of collision.*

It is very easy in bad weather when there is a lot of spray, especially at night, to be blind to things forward of the boat. There is also a temptation when self steering is used, to abandon the helm. It is vital in both of these situations that a good and adequate look-out be kept. In fog when visibility is lost, a good hearing watch should be kept. At night the helmsman may be temporarily blinded by thoughtless use of the cabin lights or matches struck close to him.

RULE 7 RISK OF COLLISION

(d) *In determining if risk of collision exists the following considerations shall be among those taken into account:*
  (i) *such risk shall be deemed to exist if the compass bearing of an approaching vessel does not appreciably change; (ii) such risk may sometimes exist even when an appreciable bearing change is evident, particularly when approaching a very large vessel or a tow or when approaching a vessel at close range.*

RULE 8 ACTION TO AVOID COLLISION

(b) *Any alteration of course and/or speed to avoid collision shall, if the circumstances*

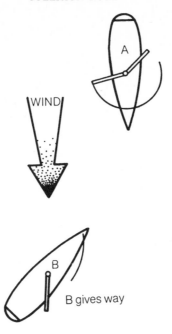

**Fig 16.1** Rule 12 (iii) Sailing Vessels. Because vessel B cannot clearly see which tack vessel A is on (the spinnaker blocks her view of A's mainsail) she must assume that A is on starboard, and B therefore has to give way, since she is on port tack. Had B been on starboard tack, she would hold her course under Rule 12 (ii).

*of the case admit, be large enough to be readily apparent to another vessel observing visually or by radar; a succession of small alterations of course and/or speed should be avoided.*

A small alteration of course by the give way vessel may not be seen by the other vessel, a series of small alterations will be confusing, possibly causing a collision. Any alteration to be made should be bold and made in plenty of time.

RULE 9 NARROW CHANNELS

*(a) A vessel proceeding along the course of a narrow channel or fairway shall keep as near to the outer limit of the channel or fairway which lies on her starboard side as is safe and practicable.*
*(b) A vessel of less than 20 metres in length or a sailing vessel shall not impede the passage of a vessel which can safely navigate only within a narrow channel or fairway.*
*(c) A vessel engaged in fishing shall not impede the passage of any other vessel navigating within a narrow channel or fairway.*
*(d) A vessel shall not cross a narrow channel or fairway if such crossing impedes the passage of a vessel which can safely navigate only within such channel or fairway. The*

*latter vessel may use the sound signal prescribed in Rule 34 (d) if in doubt as to the intention of the crossing vessel.*

*(e) (i) In a narrow channel or fairway when overtaking can take place only if the vessel overtaken has to take action to permit safe passing, the vessel intending to overtake shall indicate her intention by sounding the appropriate signal prescribed in Rule 34 (c) (i). The vessel to be overtaken shall, if in agreement, sound the appropriate signal prescribed in Rule 34 (c) (ii) and take steps to permit safe passing. If in doubt she may sound the signals prescribed in Rule 34 (d).*

*(ii) This Rule does not relieve the overtaking vessel of her obligation under Rule 13.*

*(f) A vessel nearing a bend or an area of a narrow channel or fairway where other vessels may be obscured by an intervening obstruction shall navigate with particular alertness and caution and shall sound the appropriate signal prescribed in Rule 34 (e).*

*(g) Any vessel shall, if the circumstances of the case admit, avoid anchoring in a narrow channel.*

As no definition of a 'narrow channel' is given the appropriate action depends upon the type and size of vessels using the channel.

Generally speaking, there is usually enough depth of water for a sailing vessel to navigate outside a buoyed channel used by deep draught vessels.

RULE 10 TRAFFIC SEPARATION SCHEMES

(c) *A vessel shall so far as practicable avoid crossing traffic lanes, but if obliged to do so shall cross as nearly as practicable at right angles to the general direction of traffic flow.*

If a small boat is compelled to cross a traffic separation zone, this should be done as quickly as possible with the course at right angles to the traffic flow even if this means motoring. These traffic lanes, used by very large vessels, are shown on the appropriate chart and should be studied carefully (see practice chart).

RULE 12 SAILING VESSELS

(a) *When two sailing vessels are approaching one another, so as to involve risk of collision, one of them shall keep out of the way of the other as follows:*

(i) *When each has the wind on a different side, the vessel which has the wind on the port side shall keep out of the way of the other;*

(ii) *When both have the wind on the same side, the vessel which is to windward shall keep out of the way of the vessel which is to leeward;*

(iii) *If a vessel with the wind on the port side sees a vessel to windward and cannot determine with certainty whether the other vessel has the wind on the port or on the starboard side, she shall keep out of the way of the other.*

The boat to windward may have a large sail such as a spinnaker blanketing a view of the other sails. In this rule the give way boat is on port tack, and, as she cannot determine which tack the other boat is on, it must be assumed that it is on starboard and has right of way. Had the leeward boat been on starboard tack she would have held her course and speed as the windward rule (ii) would have applied (Fig 16.1).

### RULE 13 OVERTAKING

(a) *Notwithstanding anything contained in the Rules of this section any vessel overtaking any other shall keep out of the way of the vessel being overtaken.*

The rule states *any* vessel overtaking, which is one of several instances when sail gives way to power. The give way vessel must continue on her course until she is past and clear. As she is overtaking, the situation could go on for a long time (though it may seem to change; if a sailing boat overtakes a small motor boat and the wind suddenly dies so that the two are abreast, and then the motor boat again goes ahead, the sailing boat is *still* the give way vessel).

### RULE 14 HEAD-ON SITUATION

(a) *When two power driven vessels are meeting on reciprocal or nearly reciprocal courses so as to involve risk of collision each shall alter her course to starboard so that each shall pass on the port side of the other;* Fig 16.2(a).

### RULE 15 CROSSING SITUATION

*When two power driven vessels are crossing so as to involve risk of collision, the vessel which has the other on her own starboard side shall keep out of the way and shall, if the circumstances of the case admit, avoid crossing ahead of the other vessel;* Fig 16.2(b).

The give way vessel should alter course to starboard and pass astern of the other vessel unless she is prevented from doing so, in which case an alteration to port will have to be made which will need to be considerable if she is to avoid crossing ahead.

### RULE 16 ACTION BY GIVE-WAY VESSEL

*Every vessel which is directed to keep out of the way of another vessel shall, so far as possible, take early and substantial action to keep well clear.*

An early alteration of course and a bold one so that the intentions of the give way vessel are clear in good time.

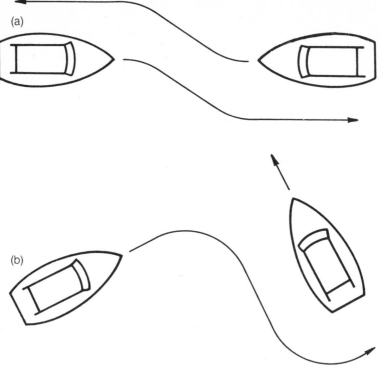

**Fig 16.2** (a) Rule 14 says that power-driven vessels meeting head on shall both turn to starboard.

(b) Rule 15, power driven-vessels crossing. The old ditty 'If to starboard Red appear, 'tis your duty to keep clear' helps to remember this rule.

RULE 17 ACTION BY STAND-ON VESSEL

(a) (i) *Where one of two vessels is to keep out of the way the other shall keep her course and speed.*

(ii) *The latter vessel may however take action to avoid collision by her manoeuvre alone, as soon as it becomes apparent to her that the vessel required to keep out of the way is not taking appropriate action in compliance with these Rules.*

(b) *When from any cause, the vessel required to keep her course and speed finds herself so close that collision cannot be avoided by the action of the give-way vessel alone, she shall take such action as will best aid to avoid collision.*

(c) *A power-driven vessel which takes action in a crossing situation in accordance with sub-paragraph (a) (ii) of this Rule to avoid collision with another power-driven vessel shall, if the circumstances of the case admit, not alter course to port for a vessel on her own port side.*

(d) *This Rule does not relieve the give-way vessel of her obligation to keep out of the way.*

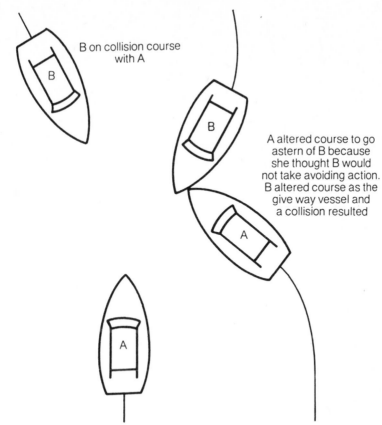

B on collision course
with A

A altered course to go
astern of B because
she thought B would
not take avoiding action.
B altered course as the
give way vessel and
a collision resulted

**Fig 16.3** How things can go wrong under Rule 17.

In Fig 16.3 vessel A has right of way but is not sure whether vessel B will take avoiding action. If vessel A decides that she must alter course to avoid collision and does so to port, B may suddenly decide that as give way vessel she will take avoiding action, and if she also alters course to port to pass behind A a collision will result. A better course of action for A if she must take avoiding action would be to stop or go astern, or turn to starboard.

RULE 18 RESPONSIBILITIES BETWEEN VESSELS

*Except where Rules 9, 10 and 13 otherwise require:*
(a) *A power-driven vessel underway shall keep out of the way of:*
  (i) *a vessel not under command;*
  (ii) *a vessel restricted in her ability to manoeuvre;*
  (iii) *a vessel engaged in fishing;*
  (iv) *a sailing vessel.*

(b) *A sailing vessel underway shall keep out of the way of:*
   (i) *a vessel not under command;*
   (ii) *a vessel restricted in her ability to manoeuvre;*
   (iii) *a vessel engaged in fishing.*

(c) *A vessel engaged in fishing when underway shall so far as possible, keep out of the way of;*
   (i) *a vessel not under command;*
   (ii) *a vessel restricted in her ability to manoeuvre.*

(d) (i) *Any vessel other than a vessel not under command or a vessel restricted in her ability to manoeuvre shall, if the circumstances of the case admit, avoid impeding the safe passage of a vessel constrained by her draught, exhibiting the signals in Rule 28;*
   (ii) *A vessel constrained by her draught shall navigate with particular caution having full regard to her special condition.*

(e) *A seaplane on the water shall, in general, keep well clear of all vessels and avoid impeding their navigation. In circumstances, however, where risk of collision exists, she shall comply with the Rules of this Part.*


Sailing vessels must also keep clear when they are the overtaking vessel whether they are overtaking power or sail, and must not impede any vessel which has a deep draught and cannot navigate outside her channel.

The signals (in Rule 28) exhibited by a vessel constrained by her draught are: three all round red lights in a vertical line, or a cylinder.


RULE 19 CONDUCT OF VESSELS IN RESTRICTED VISIBILITY

(a) *This Rule applies to vessels not in sight of one another when navigating in or near an area of restricted visibility.*

(b) *Every vessel shall proceed at a safe speed adapted to the prevailing circumstances and conditions of restricted visibility. A power driven vessel shall have her engines ready for immediate manoeuvre.*

(c) *Every vessel shall have due regard to the prevailing circumstances and conditions of restricted visibility when complying with the Rules of Section 1 of this Part.*

(d) *A vessel which detects by radar alone the presence of another vessel shall determine if a close-quarter situation is developing and/or risk of collision exists. If so, she shall take avoiding action in ample time, provided that when such action consists of an alteration of course so far as possible the following shall be avoided:*
   (i) *an alteration of course to port for a vessel forward of the beam, other than for a vessel being overtaken.*
   (ii) *an alteration of course towards a vessel abeam or abaft the beam.*

(e) *Except where it has been determined that a risk of collision does not exist, every vessel which hears apparently forward of her beam the fog signal of another vessel, or which cannot avoid a close-quarters situation with another vessel forward of her beam, shall reduce her speed to the minimum at which she can be kept on her course. She shall if necessary take all her way off and in any event navigate with extreme caution until danger of collision is over.*

Great care is necessary by small boats caught in fog, see pages 151 to 157.

### RULE 37 DISTRESS SIGNALS

*When a vessel is in distress and requires assistance she shall use or exhibit the signals prescribed in Annex IV to these regulations.*

*Annex IV*
1. *The following signals, used or exhibited either together or separately, indicate distress and need of assistance:*
(a) *a gun or other explosive signal fired at intervals of about a minute;*
(b) *a continuous sounding with any fog-signalling apparatus;*
(c) *rockets or shells, throwing red stars fired one at a time at short intervals.*
(d) *a signal made by radiotelegraphy or by any other signalling method consisting of the group · · · – – – · · · (SOS) in the Morse Code;*
(e) *a signal sent by radiotelephony consisting of the spoken word 'Mayday';*
(f) *The International Code Signal of distress indicated by NC;*
(g) *a signal consisting of a square flag having above or below it a ball or anything resembling a ball;*
(h) *flames on the vessel (as from a burning tar barrel, oil barrel, etc);*
(i) *a rocket parachute flare or a hand flare showing a red light;*
(j) *a smoke signal giving off orange-coloured smoke;*
(k) *slowly and repeatedly raising and lowering arms outstretched to each side;*
(l) *the radio telegraph alarm signal;*
(m) *the radiotelephone alarm signal;*
(n) *signals transmitted by emergency position-indicating radio beacons.*

2. *The use or exhibition of any of the foregoing signals except for the purpose of indicating distress and need of assistance and the use of other signals which may be confused with any of the above signals is prohibited.*

3. *Attention is drawn to the relevant sections of the International Code of Signals, the Merchant Ship Search and Rescue Manual and the following signals;   (a) a piece of orange coloured canvas with either a black square and circle or other appropriate symbol (for identification from the air);*
    (b) *a dye marker.*

*Flares.* Pin point red hand flare is for use when within three miles of land or near other boats; it burns bright red for 1 minute. Red parachute rocket is for long range situations when a hand flare would not be seen below the horizon, it projects a very bright parachute flare to over 300m and burns for 40 seconds. Rockets turn into the wind, so aim vertically or 15°

downwind if the wind is strong. Should there be low cloud the angle should be increased to 45° downwind, so that the rocket will be seen under the cloud base. Initially fire two flares with a one minute interval between.

*Orange Smoke Signal.* Hand held orange smoke signal produces a cloud of orange smoke for 40 seconds for use when within sight of help; for further offshore a buoyant orange smoke which burns for 3 minutes should be used. These show up very well from the air, but in strong winds may be dispersed blown along the sea surface and not easily distinguished from sea level.

*Recommended Packs.* No more than 3 miles offshore: 2 red hand flares and two hand held orange smoke signals. Between 3–7 miles offshore: 2 red parachute rockets, two red handflares, two hand held orange smoke signals. More than 7 miles offshore: 4 red parachute flares, four red hand held flares, two buoyant orange smoke signals.

*Care.* Stow flares in a dry place in a waterproof container where they are readily accessible, replace when expiry date is reached and dispose of the old ones by weighting and sinking in *deep* water. Should a flare fail to fire, keep in the firing position for at least thirty seconds and then remove the end caps and throw into the sea. See that everyone on board knows how to operate all pyrotechnics carried and follow the manufacturers' instructions.

*Flags.* If flags are used they will not be distinguished up or downwind, and are only of used when within sight of help.

*Shapes.* Again these are only of use if within sight of someone.

*Radio Telephony Distress Procedure.* This is explained on page 129.

# QUESTION PAPER 16 – COLLISION RULES

Answers on page 194

16.1  When must a good look out be kept?

16.2  If compelled to cross a traffic separation zone, how should this be done?

16.3  Where will details of traffic separation zones be found?

16.4  Which of the following boats has right of way?

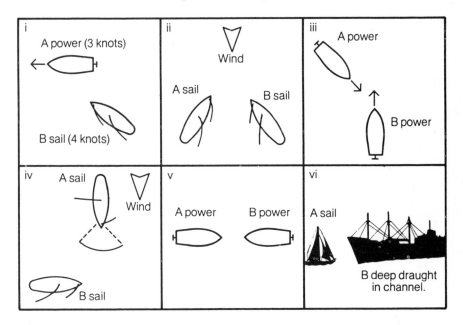

16.5  Boat A is entering the river. What is wrong with her position?

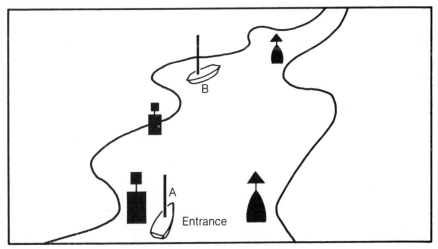

16.6   How can boat B tell whether she is on a collision course with boat A?

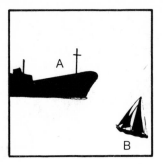

*Chapter Seventeen*

# Passage Planning

## Preparation

A lot of preparation can be done before the actual day of the passage. For a week before the passage, the weather should be studied, building all available information daily into a chart to show the general trend so that, if necessary, due to severe weather conditions, final arrangements can be modified with adequate notice.

All charts which are likely to be needed should be put in order of use in a folder. Always have the largest scale available for harbour entrances, anchorages, areas where it is required to take fixes or negotiate hazards, and a small scale chart showing the whole passage. See that they are all corrected to date and that the latest *Notices to Mariners* is on board.

Check that all the required sailing directions, nautical almanac, tide tables, tidal stream atlas and other books used are on board.

Check all safety equipment, engine, supplies, fuel, water, cooking fuel, and if the boat has not been used regularly a general check of the whole equipment is necessary, seeing that things like winches are in working order or that sails are in a good state of repair and can be hoisted without trouble.

If the crew are unfamiliar with the boat, it is a good idea to have a general briefing on the use of gear, sail hoisting, stowage, and to arrange watches and cooking duties so that everyone knows well in advance what is expected of them.

Plot the proposed courses, as even if tidal streams and wind direction cannot be allowed for, a rough idea of the proposed passage can be obtained and these courses can be used temporarily whilst a more accurate one is being plotted at the actual time. Make a plan of any clearing bearings or transits for port departure and entrance and check any local regulations.

Fill up the tidal stream atlas for the whole of the journey, and make a list of radio beacons with call signs and frequencies, buoys, lights, fog signals and anything else likely to be needed. Read the Sailing Directions to see whether it would be best to avoid any particular areas.

If the boat has not already been registered with the coastguard under the HM Coastguard Yacht and Boat Safety Scheme, this must be done.

Keep a check list.

## The Passage

Get a weather report from the local weather office, for the area of the intended passage.

Check all gear, supplies, extra fuel and see that everything is well stowed in case of bad weather.

Check all the boat safety equipment and see that everyone knows where it is stowed and how to use it. Issue personal safety equipment and, if necessary, adjust this to fit each crew member.

Plot the first leg of the course and decide upon a starting time. If sailing to windward it will only be possible to estimate the best course the helmsman can steer initially.

Have an alternative plan prepared ready for all emergencies.

Before sailing, leave word with your shore contact, and the coastguard if intending to sail outside coastal waters.

Keep entries in the boat's log hourly, and when alterations of course occur or conditions change. The log is an important document for providing information regarding the passage for later reference. It is also useful as a record should the same passage be attempted a second time. Include in the log the number of hours the engine runs, as this is required for maintainance purposes.

Always take into account the seaworthiness of the boat and the experience or lack of experience of the crew, and do not hesitate to cancel or curtail the passage at any point if in doubt regarding weather conditions, or for any reason where the safety of the boat or her crew may be at risk.

DECK LOG (OR BOAT'S LOG)

This can be merely an exercise book ruled off into columns, but there are many ready made versions and the final choice is personal. It should include such information as, wind speed and direction, barometric trend, buoyage, alterations to course and speed, general weather, distance between courses, position and time of fixes (this is very useful if a sudden fog descends), and the date.

Some navigators prefer to keep a rough log which can be used on deck, and transfer the information later to the proper boat's log. Keeping a deck log is a legal requirement for non-pleasure vessels over 25 tons.

UK CUSTOMS REGULATIONS

Full details are published in Notice No 8 obtained from HM Customs and

Excise; briefly the requirements are as follows:

Notice of departure must be given on Part I of form C1328 to the nearest Customs Office, and Immigration must be informed if there is any person on board who does not have the right of abode in UK. Upon arrival, flag Q (suitably illuminated if it is dark) must be flown when entering UK territorial waters. A full report or a quick report may be made: if any of the conditions laid down in Notice No 8 apply, a full report must be made; or if none of these conditions apply, a quick report may be made.

In either case, when the boat arrives at her destination, she must notify the nearest Customs Office within 2 hours. If a full report is to be made, she then awaits the arrival of the Customs Officer. If a quick report is to be made, she awaits the arrival of the Customs Officer, and if the boat has not been visited within 2 hours after notification, Part II of form C1328 is completed and posted to the Customs Office where notification of arrival was given. The members of the boat may then leave.

FOREIGN CUSTOMS

Whereas in ECC countries procedure may be similar, there are variations, and local regulations should be studied before entry, especially as they change periodically. Some countries require a Helmsman's Certificate of Competence.

It is customary, but not essential in some countries, to fly flag Q until cleared by customs.

If a boat is registered, the registration papers should be carried when going foreign as these are needed in some countries.

FLAG ETIQUETTE

A cruising yacht is properly dressed flying both a masthead burgee and an ensign.

*Burgee.* This is usually the burgee of the club or association to which the owner or skipper belongs, and should be flown at all times when the boat is in commission and the owner or skipper on board or close ashore and in effective control.

*Ensign.* This is normally the Red Ensign. Other ensigns (white, blue, blue defaced, red defaced) can be flown if authorised by a special warrant and only if the owner and warrant are on board (in conjunction with the correct burgee). At sea, the ensign is flown at all times, but in harbour it is hoisted at colours (i.e. 0800 summer, 0900 winter), and lowered at sunset. In the event of the boat being unmanned at these times, the ensign should be hoisted or lowered at the earliest and latest opportunity. When passing a warship of any nationality it is courteous to dip the ensign until the warship has responded by dipping and hoisting hers.

*Courtesy Ensign.* In a foreign country the ensign of that country should be flown from the starboard spreader from the time of arrival in their territorial waters to the time of departure.

### 'M' NOTICES

These are notices issued by the Department of Transport, obtainable free from Mercantile Marine Offices. They are Merchant Shipping Notices, but often contain information of use to small boats such as: fire prevention, calibration of radio equipment, storage of portable water, use of radio telephone by unskilled persons, carriage of dangerous goods, effects of radio on magnetic compasses, medical procedures and precautions, international code of signals, pollution control, keeping a safe navigational watch, standard marine navigational vocabulary, towing, lifesaving appliances.

They do not give any information on navigation which is included in Admiralty *Notices to Mariners*.

## TEST PAPERS FOLLOW ON NEXT PAGE

# TEST PAPER A – COASTAL NAVIGATION

Answers on page 195 to 199
Extract on page 70

This exercise concerns the passage of a boat from Newhaven to Rye on 7th October 1980. The boat is a bilge keel auxiliary sloop, LOA 8m, draught 1·4m. Use the deviation table Fig 4.4 and 6°W variation. All times BST.

A.1   Before making the passage, what action should the skipper have taken to ensure that in the event of non-arrival at the destination, appropriate action may be initiated?

A.2   In addition to the BBC Shipping Forecast, how could the expected weather for the duration of the passage be checked?

A.3   The shipping forecast at 0033 for sea area Dover was SE 3-4 backing E 4–5 later, visibility good becoming moderate. Sunrise is at 0710 and sunset at 1826.
   (a) What considerations should be taken into account before deciding upon the best time to sail for Rye, assuming the boat's speed is 4 knots?
   (b) What would be the best time to sail for Rye?

A.4   On leaving Newhaven, the best course steered to windward on port tack is found to be 195°C. Closehauled the boat makes a course 45° off the wind, leeway is 5°, tidal stream 090°T, 1.5 knots, visibility 10 miles. When should the boat tack to lay a course to clear the overfalls South of Beachy head?

A.5   At 0900 log reading 10·6, the following bearings were taken using the hand bearing compass:

Wish tower on Eastbourne seafront
     in transit with gasholder         025°M
Royal Sovereign lighthouse        091°M

   (a) Plot the 0900 position.
   (b) Is this fix accurate?

A.6   At 0900 a course was set to pass between the Royal Sovereign Lighthouse and the red buoy to the South of Royal Sovereign shoals. Estimated leeway 5°. Assume the boat can make a direct course at a speed of 4 knots.
   (a) What is the course to steer?
   (b) What time will Royal Sovereign Lighthouse be abeam?

A.7   At 1010 log reading 15·3, the boat leaves the red buoy close abeam to port and sets course for the landfall buoy (RW LFl 10s) in Rye Bay. Leeway is negligible.
  (a)  What is the course to steer?
  (b)  What is the estimated time of arrival at the landfall buoy?

A.8   At 1110 log reading 19·2, the following bearings were taken:

| | |
|---|---|
| Tower in Bexhill | 338°M |
| White house on St Leonards sea front | 014°M |
| Tower inshore of Fairlight village | 039°M |

  (a)  Plot the 1110 position.
  (b)  Is the tidal stream experienced between 1010 and 1110 as expected?

A.9   Why were the following not used for taking bearings to obtain a position line?
  (a)  The dome of the Royal Greenwich Observatory.
  (b)  The yellow buoy (FIY 5s) off St Leonards.

A.10   At 1130 the visibility appears to be getting worse and the wind starts backing towards the east. What action should the boat take?

# TEST PAPER B – OFFSHORE PASSAGE MAKING

Answers on page 200-2
Extracts on page 70

This exercise concerns a passage from Calais to Dover on 7th September. The boat is a fin keel sloop LOA 12m draught 1.9m. The wind is forecast ENE 3–4. Sunrise is at 0621 and sunset at 1935. Use the deviation table Fig 4.4 and 6°W variation. All times given are BST.

B.1   Having left Calais at 0315 a good passage has been made on a course for Dover. At 0458 a light FlR 20s is raised on a bearing of 284°M with a height of eye of 1·5m.
   (a)  Plot the boat's position at 0458.
   (b)  What course should be set for Dover from this position?
The following table shows the approximate distance of the sea horizon in nautical miles for various heights of eye:

| Ht of eye in metres | Distance off in miles |
|---|---|
| 1·5 | 2·6 |
| 10·0 | 6·6 |
| 11·0 | 7·0 |
| 12·0 | 7·2 |
| 13·0 | 7·5 |
| 14·0 | 7·8 |

B.2   The following is an extract from the boat's log:

| Time | Log | Course | Remarks |
|---|---|---|---|
| 0458 | 8·4 | 314°C | Fix on Varne Lightvessel. |
| 0600 | 13·7 | 314°C | wind dropped to force 2-3, no leeways visibility 7–8 miles. |
| 0640 | 16·9 | 314°C | visibility dropped to 3–4 miles; Varne Lightvessel bearing 223°M. |
| 0700 | 18·5 | 314°C | Varne Lightvessel bearing 183°M; wind dropped to force 2. |

   (a)  Plot the position of the boat at 0700.
   (b)  Does this position agree with the EP for 0700?
   (c)  What is the course to steer from this position for the East Entrance of Dover Harbour, assuming the engine is started and the boat maintains a speed of 5 knots?

B.3   Visibility continues to drop and is estimated to be about 1 mile:
   (a)  List the precautions to be taken.
   (b)  Are there any particular navigational hazards due to the restricted visibility?
At 0700 the course steered is 000°C.

B.4   At 0730 log reading 21·1, the echo sounder (which is a LED rotating dial type, set on its lowest scale with a full scale reading of 20 metres) indicated at depth of 3 metres. Comment on this reading.

B.5   At 0740 the boat sights the east end of the detached breakwater and sets course to enter the outer harbour. On sighting the south end of the eastern breakwater, a signal consisting of 3 red balls in a triangle is observed. Where could the meaning of this signal be found and what might it mean?

B.6   Having entered the outer harbour it is decided, because of the visibility, to anchor off the shore in front of the castle. Having anchored at 0827 the depth of water is found to be 4·8m.
   (a)  How much anchor chain should be veered (let out)?
   (b)  What will be the minimum clearance under the keel in the next 12 hours?

# Answers to Questions and Test Papers

**CHAPTER 1**

1.1 **1:150,000.** This means that 150,000 units measured on the land or sea will be represented by one unit on the chart.

1.2   (a) **Small scale charts** for planning the whole passage.
    (b) **Larger scale** for. congested waters.
    (c) **Largest scale** for port entrance and anchorages.
    (d) **Tide Tables.**
    (e) **Tidal Stream Atlas.**
    (f) **Admiralty List of Radio Services for Small Craft.**
    (g) Relevant **Notices to Mariners.**
    (h) **Sailing Directions.**
    (i) One of the **commerical almanacs.**

1.3   (a) Admiralty catalogue **NP 131.**
    (b) **Notices to Mariners, Annual or Small Craft Edition.**

1.4 These are **warnings giving the location of the hazard concerned** and should be read before using the chart.

1.5 **Chart 5011 Symbols and Abbreviations.**

1.6 Details of **land features, tidal notes, dangers, weather information, port entrance** and other items to facilitate safe navigation.

1.7   (a) *Stanfords.* By **returning to them,** or obtaining a list of corrections.
    (b) *Imray.* By obtaining the **bulletin** or the **correction slips** which are periodically available, or by **returning to them.**
    (c) *Admiralty.* **Notices to Mariners, weekly edition** (with annual summary), free from Mercantile Marine Offices, Customs Houses and Chart Agents or **Notices to Mariners, Small Craft Edition,** from Chart Agents, nautical booksellers etc. for which a small charge is made.

1.8 The **appropriate chart catalogue:**
    (a) Admiralty charts, *NP 131* or *NP 109* limited edition
    (b) Stanford and Imray charts, the firm's own catalogue.

1.9 The **Small Craft Edition of Notices to Mariners** is only published quarterly and so may be out of date, but as it summarises corrections to home waters charts it saves a lot of searching through weekly notices.

10.10 **Metres and decimetres.**

## CHAPTER 2

2.1　**A circle, the plane of which passes through the centre of a sphere**, dividing it into two equal portions. The equator is a great circle.

2.2　**A rhumb line cuts all meridians on the earth's surface at the same angle**. It appears on a mercator projection chart as a straight line but on a gnomonic projection chart as a curve.

2.3　**Because one minute of longitude is not equal to one minute of latitude except on the equator.** The latitude scale constantly varies, increasing in length towards the poles, and one minute of latitude at the bottom of a chart (for north latitude) will not measure as much as one minute of latitude at the top of the chart. The longitude scale cannot be used for measurement but only as a reference point.

2.4　(a) **30° 2'·1N**

　　　(b) **2° 6'·8W**

2.5 ·**Because the distortion caused by this type of projection becomes infinite**, and therefore a gnomonic projection is used for polar regions.

## CHAPTER 3

3.1　**040°T.**

3.2　(a) **51° 1'·3N, 1° 24'·0E**

　　　(b) **50° 55'·7N, 1° 17'·3E**

　　　(c) **50° 55'·9N, 1° 37'·6E**

3.3　**293°T.**

3.4　**065°T**

3.5　⟨Ė⟩

## CHAPTER 4

4.1　**The line on the fixed part of the compass which is positioned on the fore and aft line of the boat.**

4.2　Printed **on the line across the compass rose** on the chart for that area, or **on a magnetic chart**.

4.3　(a) **In the fore and aft line of the boat.**

　　　(b) **Well away from magnetic influences.**

　　　(c) **Where it will suffer no damage.**

　　　(d) **Visible from the steering position.**

　　　(e) **Preferably with an all round view of the horizon.**

　　　(f) **Firmly secured.**

4.4　(a) **028°T**

　　　(b) **292°T**

　　　(c) **130°T**

4.5　Deviation is for the boat's heading and will be the same for all bearings:

| heading | | 315°C |
|---|---|---|
| deviation | = | 5°E + |
| | | 320°M |
| variation | = | 6°W − |
| | | 314°T |

　　　(compass error = 1°W)

True bearings are:
  (a) **114°T**
  (b) **150°T**
  (c) **218°T**
4.6  The hand bearing compass is **not used in exactly the same place every time**.
4.7  (a) **043°M** (2°W).
    (b) **216½°M** (2½°E).
    (c) **313½°M** (1½°W).

## CHAPTER 5  (see plots)

5.1  **51° 4'·7N, 1° 16'·2E**
5.2  **50° 59'·2N, 1° 5'·1E** Water track 245 T
5.3  **50° 52'·8N, 0° 49'·9E** Water track 279 T

|                  Tidal streams        |     Interpolation     |
| ------------------------------------- | --------------------- |
| 5 hours before HW 211° T, 1·2 knots   |                       |
|                                       | 211°, 1·1 knots       |
| 4 hours before HW 211° T, 1·1 knots   |                       |
|                                       | 211°, 0·8 knots       |
| 3 hours before HW 211° T, 0·5 knots   |                       |

## CHAPTER 6  (see plots)

6.1  (a) **075°T.**
    (b) **2 hours 38 minutes.**
6.2  (a) **062°T.**
    (b) **50° 52'·5N, 0° 57'·6E.**
    (c) **0956.**
    (d) **6·3 knots.**
6.3  (a) **351°T.**
    (b) **1847**
The vector diagrams for questions 2 and 3 are for a period of 2 and 3 hours respectively, because in both these instances it is easier to draw the vectors (which represent speeds) for a whole number of hours, making appropriate allowances for the small differences obtained for distance travelled and time taken.

## CHAPTER 7  (see plots)

7.1  (a) **10m**
    (b) **2°W**
Horizontal angles 55° and 28°.
Angles to plot 35° and 62° (if using construction method).
**Position 50° 52'·8N, 0° 51'·6E**

|                                        |          |
| -------------------------------------- | -------- |
| True bearing of tower (20)             | 343°T    |
| variation =                            | 6°W      |
|                                        | 349°M    |
| deviation =                            | 2°W      |
|                                        | 351°C    |

**Figs A 5.1, A 5.2,** and **A 5.3.** The lat and long would normally be taken from the edge of the chart, but you can transfer them to a convenient point for working purposes.

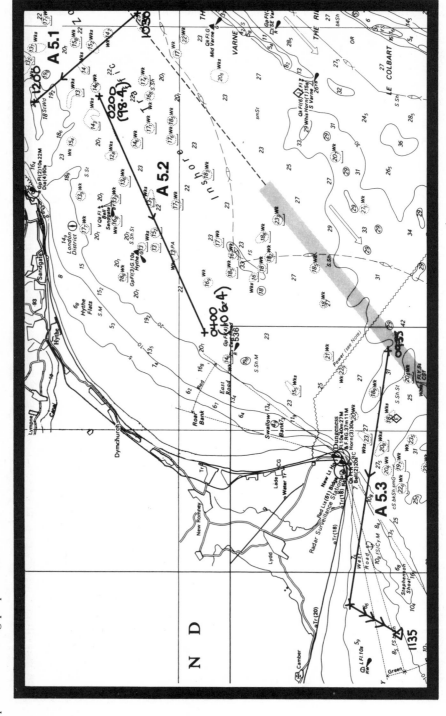

Fig A 6.1

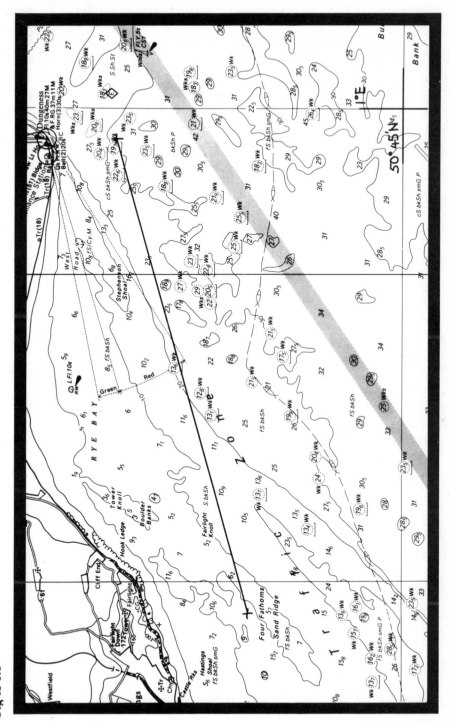

Fig A 6.2

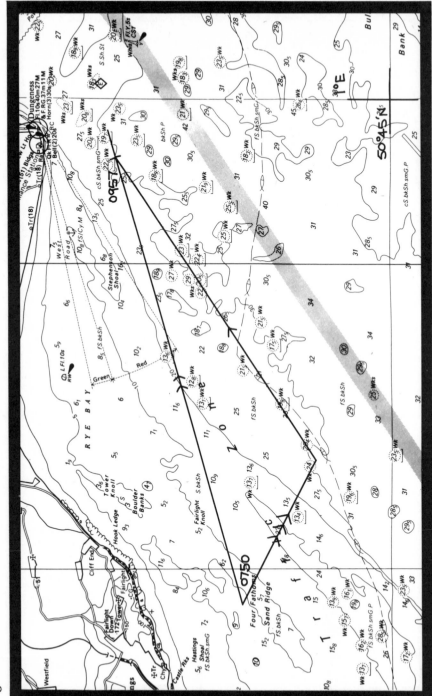

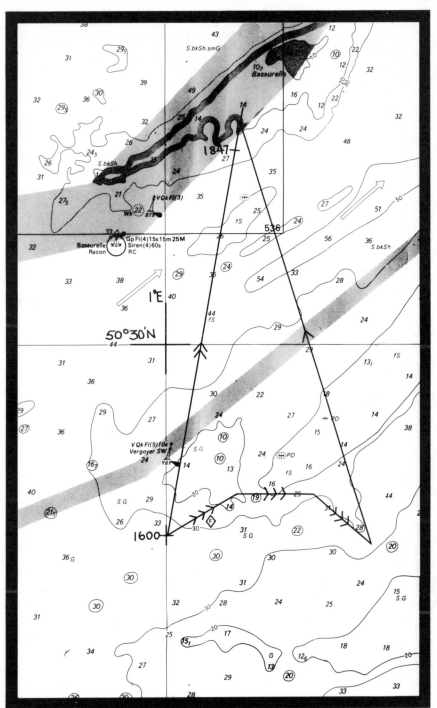

Fig A 6.3

Fig A 7.1

**Fig A 7.2/4**

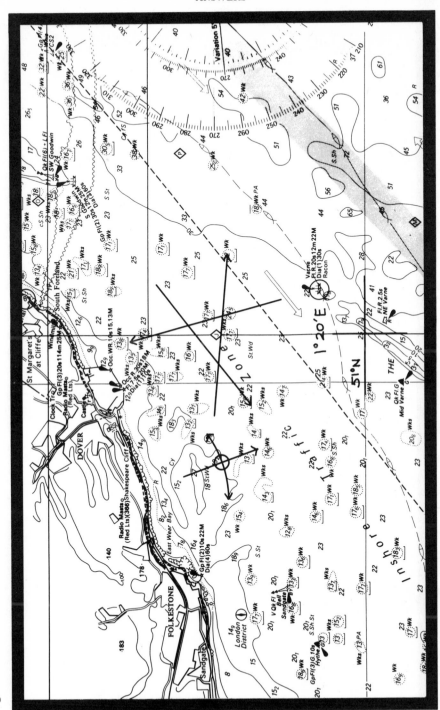

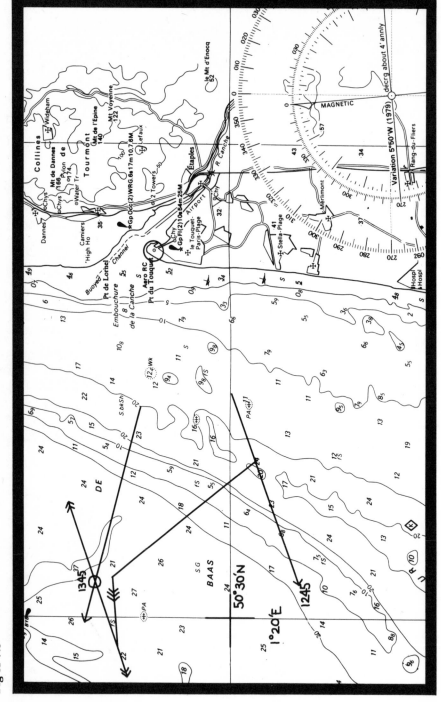

Fig A 7.3

7.2  (a) **51° 03'·9N, 1° 16'·6E.**
    (b) **20m**

$$\text{Distance off in miles} = \frac{\text{Ht of object in metres} \times 1·854}{\text{VSA in minutes}}$$

$$\frac{366 \times 1·854}{226} = 3 \text{ miles}$$

7.3  **50° 33'·8N, 1° 21'·7E.**

7.4  **Not satisfactory** because of the large cocked hat, bearings would need to be checked.


## CHAPTER 8

8.1

| | |
|---|---|
| Drying height | 1·5m |
| Draught | +2·1m |
| Clearance | +0.5m |
| Height of tide | 4·1m |

8.2(a)

| | HW | | LW | |
|---|---|---|---|---|
| | time | height | time | height |
| Portsmouth | **0233 BST** | **4.4m** | **0750 BST** | **0.9m** |
| | **1507 BST** | **4.5m** | **2009 BST** | **1.2m** |
| (b)  **Ranges:** | **3.5m**  **3.3m** | | | |
| (c) | **0.71 from a neap tide** | | | |
| | **0.62 from a neap tide** | | | |

(Portsmouth mean ranges: spring 4.1m, neap 2.0m)

8.3

| | HW | | LW | | range |
|---|---|---|---|---|---|
| | time | height | time | height | |
| Dover | 2217 BST | 6.4m | 1737 BST | 1.1m | 5.3m |
| | | | | | (0.3 from springs) |

| | |
|---|---|
| Time Required | 2015 BST |
| Interval | 2h 02m before HW |
| HW Dover | 2217 BST |
| **Height** | **4.7m** |

8.4

| | |
|---|---|
| Height of Dungeness light above MHWS | 40m |
| MHWS Dover = 6.7m, corrected for Dungeness | +8m |
| Height of light above CD | **48m** |

8.5(a)

| | HW | | LW | |
|---|---|---|---|---|
| | height | time | height | range |
| Portsmouth | 4.9m | 0529 GMT | 0.4m | 4.5m |
| Differences | −3.0m | −0035 | −0.0 | (Spring) |
| Christchurch | 1.9m | 0454 GMT | 0.4m | |
| | | 0554 BST | | |

| | |
|---|---|
| Time Required | 0400 BST |
| Interval | 1h 54m before LW |
| **Height** | **1.1m** |

8.6

| | HW | | LW | |
|---|---|---|---|---|
| | time | height | height | range |
| Dover | 2306 GMT | 6.5m | 1.2m | 5.3 |
| Differences | +0020 | −1.8m | −0.5m | (0.3 from |
| | | | | springs) |
| Ramsgate | 2326 GMT | 4.7m | 0.7m | |

| | |
|---|---|
| Height Required | 4.0m |
| Interval | 1h 30m before HW |
| HW Ramsgate | 2326 GMT |
| **Time** | **2156 GMT** |

## CHAPTER 9

9.1 **See plot.**

9.2 (a) Radiation fog **in winter time** when the nights are long and cold then adequate cooling of air below its dew point can take place.

(b) Advection fog **in spring or early summer** when the sea is at its coldest and warm saturated air flows over it from warmer regions.

9.3 **Cumulus** and **cumulonimbus** of great vertical height.

9.4 (a) This is probably a **cold front approaching**; on passage the **wind will veer and increase in strength**.

(b) The boat should be ready to **tack or bear away and reef** her sails if necessary.

9.5 This could be the **approach of a warm front**.

The wind will veer, there may be some rain or frontal fog, **generally bad weather**.

9.6 This is a **sea breeze** caused by the land being warmed by the sun and warming the air on contact with it which rises. Air over the sea flows in to take the place of the rising air.

9.7 **No**, 'poor' indicates visibility of 2 miles or less.

9.8 The barometer is a good indication of forthcoming weather but needs to be watched regularly and backed up with other information for accurate results, generally speaking however:

(a) rapidly rising, this could be **the passage of a cold front** when visibility will clear and the wind veer and strengthen.

(b) fairly high and steady, could indicate **a high pressure system** with light winds and steady weather.

(c) rapidly falling then remaining steady, possibly **the approach and passage of a warm front** with bad weather expected.

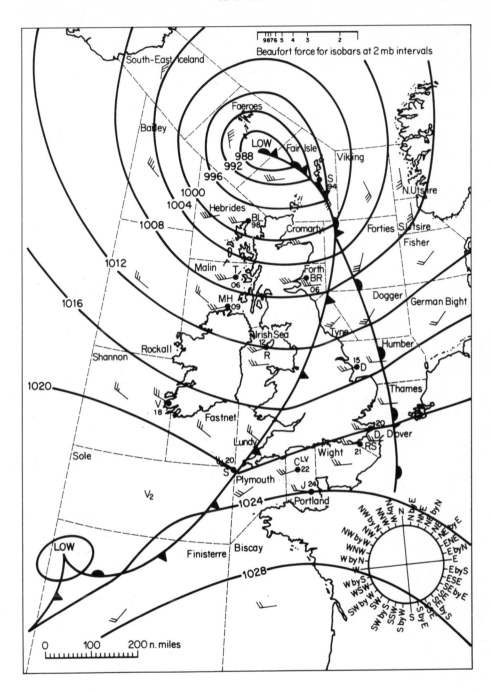

Beaufort force for isobars at 2 mb intervals

9.9   On 1500m (200 kHz) **in the shipping forecast** four times a day, also issued as soon as possible after receipt and then repeated after the next news bulletin. **By Coast Radio Stations.**

9.10   **After the cold front** where gales are frequent. Strong winds are also experienced near the centre of a depression.

## CHAPTER 10

10.1   **A trip line** should be rigged on the anchor and led back aboard the boat. By day **a round ball** should be hoisted up the forestay, and by night **a white all round light** high up in the fore part of the boat should be shown if the local regulations require this.

10.2   **Select suitable transits** or bearings of objects abeam, which will alter should the anchor drag.

10.3   **40m** (5 × 8m).

10.4   (a) **Sufficient chain or warp** for the maximum expected depth.

      (b) **Sheltered** from all expected winds.

      (c) **Out of strong tidal streams.**

      (d) **Clear of obstructions** when the boat swings.

      (e) **Sufficient water** to avoid going aground.

      (f) **Free of underwater obstructions.**

      (g) **With a suitable landing place.**

10.5   No anchor holds well on rock. **The Fisherman** is more likely to hold than the others, but can also become easily fouled.

## CHAPTER 11

11.1   (a) **Morse code, Mo(R).**

      (b) **Isophase, Iso.**

      (c) **Single flashing, Fl.**

      (d) **Single occulting, Oc.**

11.2   **South cardinal.** The danger is to the North of the buoy and so **the boat should pass to the South of the buoy**.

11.3

11.4   (a) **On starboard side.**

      (b) **On port side.**

11.5   The buoy is a west cardinal buoy and the danger is to the East. **The boat should leave it to port**.

## CHAPTER 12

12.1   **A trailing log** is the more accurate, usually giving an error of less than 2 miles.

12.2   **Switch to a larger scale.** The reading is probably a second trace, which would correspond to a depth of 37m.

12.3   By simple trigonometry, the error in position could be up to **nearly 2 miles**.

12.4   During the day **well after sunrise and well before sunset**; and **where the radio path to the beacon does not pass over high ground or cross any coastline at an oblique angle**.

12.5   **Channel 16.**

## CHAPTER 13

13.1 (a) *Safety harness*. **For foredeck work when the weather is rough, at night, when alone on the helm, at any time when there is a danger of falling overboard.**

(b) *Lifejacket*. **By non-swimmers, in fog, in the dinghy between the boat and the shore, and when possibility exists of forced abandonment.**

13.2 **Throw in the lifebelt** and the dan buoy whilst at the same time **calling 'Man Overboard'** to alert the crew. **Detail someone to point to the man and call out his position. Get the boat steady and under control ready for the pick-up.**

13.3 **Fire a red flare.**

13.4 Smother the fire by **covering with a fire blanket** or a blanket soaked in water. **Turn off the cooker.** Do not attempt to throw burning utensils overboard as spillage may cause further fires, or to throw water on a fire caused by cooking oil.

13.5 At least **two 1·5 kg dry powder or equivalent fire extinguishers**, **a fire blanket**, **a bag of sand** for oil fires and **two buckets** with strong handles and lanyards.


## CHAPTER 14

14.1 Immediately **flood the area with cold water** (by plunging into the sea if this can be done easily), for at least 10 minutes. **Cover with a clean, smooth dry cloth, seek medical help if needed.**

14.2 There is always a danger of a person who is being seasick falling over the side of the boat. If they are on deck **they should be secured to the boat** by their safety harness clip. In a severe case **they should be put down below** and made to lie down, kept warm and provided with a bucket. As soon as possible **they should be put ashore. Plenty of liquid must be given** to anyone who has been continually seasick as the body rapidly dehydrates.

14.3 **The patient could be suffering from compression,** a dangerous condition where a portion of the skull may be pressing on the brain or fluid may be collecting and compressing the brain. Their breathing should be watched and medical help obtained quickly.

14.4 **Check breathing and if necessary administer artificial resuscitation** (seconds can save a life), **treat for hypothermia and shock, attend to any other injuries (do not give food and liquids if an aneasthetic is required later), seek medical help as soon as possible.**

14.5 **Lie the patient down and treat any injury, keep the head low and turned to one side in case of vomiting so that they will not choke, loosen clothing, do not apply heat but keep warm with a blanket, reassure.**

## CHAPTER 15

15.1  **Take a fix of position, note other boats in the area, hoist radar reflector, post a good lookout well forward, put on lifejackets, sound the appropriate fog signal and considerably reduce speed.**

15.2  **Put on a safety harness and clip on to a strong point, reef the mainsail or rig the trysail, change down the foresail, check that everything above and below deck is well secured, prepare food and warm drinks, issue seasickness tablets. If possible navigate to be clear of a lee shore and try to get into sheltered waters.**

15.3  The boat should **stop or slow down** whilst the listening watch tries to ascertain where the other boat is and in which direction it is travelling. When this has been done she may **proceed but with extreme caution**, being ready to alter course immediately if required. The engine can be stopped to listen, but this leaves the boat with no means of propulsion should the engine not restart with imminent danger threatening. Far better to post a listening watch well forward.

15.4  **Heave-to** which will quieten the boat down and enable deck work to be carried out more safely.

15.5  (a) *Trysail.* **Tougher material, does not have a boom** to cause trouble so **no worry about gybing**; unless specially fitted for immediate hoisting, **the normal mainsail has to be lowered**, stowed and the boom lashed out of the way, before it can be fitted so **it can take longer than reefing the mainsail. mainsail.**

(b) *Reefing the Mainsail.* **Quicker than rigging the trysail, liable to cause wear on the sail, often does not set well but helps the boat to sail closer to the wind** than a trysail, **danger of gybing** present.


## CHAPTER 16

16.1  **At all times.**

16.2  **At right angles and as quickly as possible.** If necessary a sailing boat must use the engine.

16.3  **On the appropriate chart and in several nautical almanacs.**

16.4  (i) **A**; the overtaking boat gives way.

(ii) **B**; the starboard tack boat has right of way.

(iii) **B**; the power boat A with the other on her starboard gives way.

(iv) **A**; Boat B cannot determine which tack A is on.

(v) **Neither**; both alter course to starboard.

(vi) **B**; because she cannot navigate outside the deep draught channel as indicated by her day signal, a cylinder.

16.5  **She should keep to the right.**

16.6  **B should take frequent bearings of A** and, if they do not alter, collision is deemed to exist.

## TEST PAPER A

A.1 **The local coastguard station should have been given full details of the boat and the name of a responsible person to contact in emergency. Before the passage the skipper would ensure that this person knows the intended passage plan, and will inform the local coastguard if the skipper has not reported his safe arrival within 24 hours of his estimated time of arrival at the destination.**

A.2 **By telephoning the local forecasting station.**

A.3 The times (GMT) and heights of HW and LW at Rye are calculated as follows:

|  | HW | | | | LW | |
|---|---|---|---|---|---|---|
|  | time | height | time | height | time | height |
| Dover | 1010 | 6·4m | 2235 | 6·3m | 1734 | 1·2m |
| Differences | 0000 | 0·9m+ | 0001+ | 0·9m+ | | |
| Rye approaches | 1010 | 7·3m | 2236 | 7·2m | dries | |

|  | HW | | | | LW | |
|---|---|---|---|---|---|---|
|  | time | height | time | height | time | height |
| Dover | 1010 | 6·4m | 2235 | 6·3m | 1734 | 1·2m |
| Differences | 0000 | 1·5m− | 0001+ | 1·5m− | | |
| Rye Harbour | 1010 | 4·9m | 2336 | 4·8m | dries | |

HW at Rye Harbour is 1110 or 2336 BST.

(a) Because Rye Harbour dries out, **it would be best to enter on a rising tide**, i.e. arrive at the entrance by 1030 at the latest. However, the boat has a shallow draught and bilge keel, so she would not be particularly embarrassed if she were to dry out in an anchorage in the River Rother provided the anchorage were reasonably sheltered.

The weather forecast suggests that **a start as early as possible** should be made, so as to reach the approaches to Rye before the yacht is headed by the wind and the visibility deteriorates. Sunrise is at 0710 so **twilight will begin at about 0630** which would be the earliest time to start to make a daylight passage. The passage distance is 36 miles, which would take 9 hours at 4 knots ignoring adverse winds and tidal streams.

Off Beachy Head **the eastgoing tide** is from 5½ hours before to ½ hour after HW Dover, ie 0540 to 1140 BST. Off Dungeness it is about 4 hours later, ie 0940 to 1540 BST. It is about one third of the way from Spring tides to Neap tides (2 or 3 days after Springs), so the aggregate of the favourable tidal stream (assuming departure from Newhaven is at the beginning of the eastgoing stream), over the 9 hour passage would represent approximately 10 miles. The boat would therefore only require to sail 26 miles, which at 4 knots would take about 6½ hours; this reduces the aggregate of the tidal set but it is sufficiently accurate for initial considerations.

**Fig TA 1**

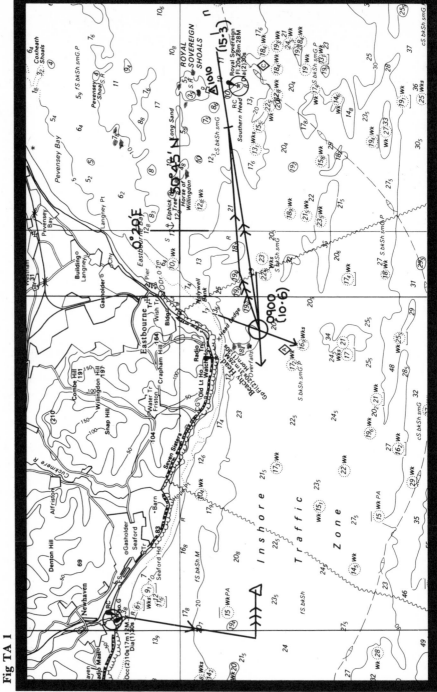

(b) From the above it is evident that **the best time to sail would be 6½ hours before 1030 ie 0400** aiming to pick up the start of the eastgoing tidal stream off Beachy Head. In the event the navigator decided to wait until twilight (0630) and until he had checked with the 0555 shipping forecast.

A.4   Course to steer on port tack                    195°C
                        deviation   =   3½°W−
                        variation   =   6°W−
True course                                           185°T (to nearest ½°)
                        leeway      =   5°+
Water track on port tack                              190°T
True course port tack                                 185°T
                                                       90°−
True course starboard tack                            095°T
                        leeway      =   5°−
Water track on starboard tack                         090°T

The tidal stream is setting effectively along the starboard tack water track, so the boat needs to tack as soon as this course would take her clear of the overfalls. This would be about 3·7 miles from Newhaven breakwater lighthouse ie 55 minutes after passing the lighthouse. In that time the tidal stream would have carried the boat 090°, 1·4 miles when Beachy Head Lighthouse would be on a bearing of 086°M. **So the time to tack would be when Beachy Head lighthouse would be on a bearing of 086°M.**

A.5   (a) **See plot** on Fig TA1 opposite
        (b) The transit of Wish Tower and the gasholder is 019°T or 025°M. This agrees with the bearings obtained from the handbearing compass, which can therefore be considered **accurate**.

A.6   (a) **See plot** on Fig TA1
        Ground track                                  081°T
        Water track                                   084°T
        Leeway                                         5°+
        True course                                   089°T
        Variation                                     6°W+
        Deviation                                      0°
        Course to steer                               **095°C**

*Estimation of tidal stream average between tidal diamonds A and C.*

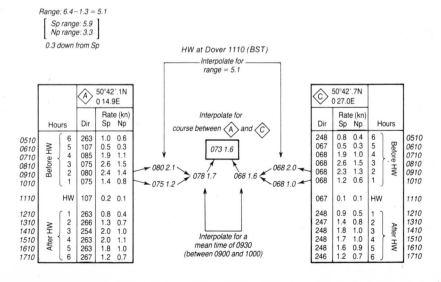

Range: 6.4−1.3 = 5.1
[ Sp range: 5.9
  Np range: 3.3 ]
0.3 down from Sp

HW at Dover 1110 (BST)
Interpolate for range = 5.1

Interpolate for course between Ⓐ and Ⓒ

| | Hours | Dir | Rate (kn) Sp | Np | | Dir | Rate (kn) Sp | Np | Hours | |
|---|---|---|---|---|---|---|---|---|---|---|
| 0510 | 6 | 263 | 1.0 | 0.6 | | 248 | 0.8 | 0.4 | 6 | 0510 |
| 0610 | 5 | 107 | 0.5 | 0.3 | | 067 | 0.5 | 0.3 | 5 | 0610 |
| 0710 | 4 | 085 | 1.9 | 1.1 | | 068 | 1.9 | 1.0 | 4 | 0710 |
| 0810 | 3 | 075 | 2.6 | 1.5 | | 068 | 2.6 | 1.5 | 3 | 0810 |
| 0910 | 2 | 080 | 2.4 | 1.4 | | 068 | 2.3 | 1.3 | 2 | 0910 |
| 1010 | 1 | 075 | 1.4 | 0.8 | | 068 | 1.2 | 0.6 | 1 | 1010 |
| 1110 | HW | 107 | 0.2 | 0.1 | | 067 | 0.1 | 0.1 | HW | 1110 |
| 1210 | 1 | 263 | 0.8 | 0.4 | | 248 | 0.9 | 0.5 | 1 | 1210 |
| 1310 | 2 | 266 | 1.3 | 0.7 | | 247 | 1.4 | 0.8 | 2 | 1310 |
| 1410 | 3 | 254 | 2.0 | 1.0 | | 248 | 1.8 | 1.0 | 3 | 1410 |
| 1510 | 4 | 263 | 2.0 | 1.1 | | 248 | 1.7 | 1.0 | 4 | 1510 |
| 1610 | 5 | 263 | 1.8 | 1.0 | | 248 | 1.6 | 0.9 | 5 | 1610 |
| 1710 | 6 | 267 | 1.2 | 0.7 | | 246 | 1.2 | 0.7 | 6 | 1710 |

Ⓐ 50°42'.1N 0 14.9E    Ⓒ 50°42'.7N 0 27.0E

Before HW / After HW

073 1.6
080 2.1
075 1.2
078 1.7
068 1.6
068 2.0
068 1.0

Interpolate for a mean time of 0930 (between 0900 and 1000)

**Fig TA 2**

(b) **See plot** on Fig TA1 speed made good 5·5 knots
distance to go 6·7 miles
time taken 1 hour 13 minutes
Estimated time Royal Sovereign lighthouse abeam **1013**.

A.7    (a) **See plot** on Fig TA2. Ground track is 055°T.
Tidal stream is difficult to estimate because of the lack of accurate data for the
areas concerned. Initially it will correspond to tidal diamond C, but as the boat
progresses, it will tend towards tidal diamond E. It will be approximately along
the track at about 0.5 knots.

| | |
|---|---|
| Course to steer | 055°T |
| Variation | 6°W + |
| Deviation | 4°E − |
| Course to steer | **057°C** |

(b) **See plot** on Fig TA2 speed made good, 4 knots boat speed
½ knot of tidal stream = 4½ knots.
Distance to go 17 miles
Time taken 3 hours 47 minutes
Estimated time of arrival at landfall buoy **1400** approximately.

A.8    (a) **See plot** on Fig TA2
(b) Estimated tidal stream **086°, 0·8 knots**: this would appear to be roughly
correct, though a direction of 068° would be expected. The opportunity should be
taken to check the direction and rate of the tidal stream by regular fixes and by
observation of buoys marking lobster pots etc.

A.9    (a) **The Dome of the Royal Greenwich Observatory may well be
obscured by land and is nearly 10 miles away, so any error in the
bearing will have more effect than objects that are closer.**
(b) **The yellow buoy is the nearest object, but it is unlikely to be visible
at nearly 3 miles distant. (Buoys can be out of position and can easily
be wrongly identified).**

A.10    The consequences of the late start are now evident. It is already past HW at
Rye and will take a further 2½ hours to reach the landfall buoy. The wind is going
ahead which makes continuing to the East extremely difficult, especially as there
are no other safe harbours for boats before Dover. As there is plenty of daylight
left, and the tidal stream has turned Westwards around Royal Sovereign
lighthouse, **the only reasonable action is to return to Newhaven**.

ANSWERS TO TEST PAPER B ON NEXT PAGE

**Fig TB 1**

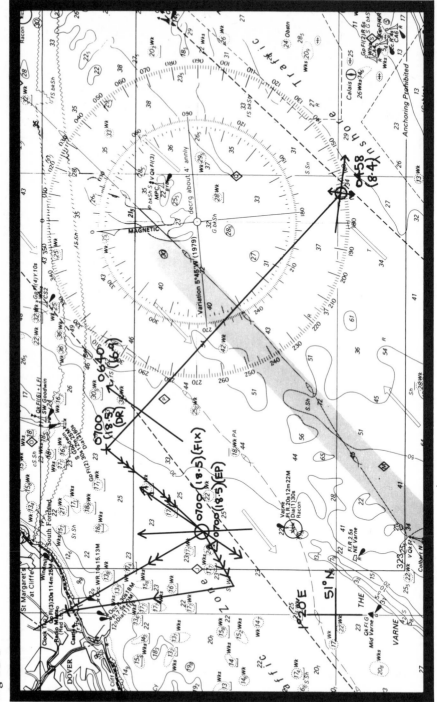

**TEST PAPER B**

B.1   (a) **See plot** on Fig TB1 opposite. The height of the light on Varne Lightvessel is 12m which, from the table, would be visible from the horizon at a distance of 7·2 miles. From the boat the horizon is 2·6 miles distant, so the lightvessel must be 9·8 miles from the boat.

(b) **A course direct to Dover cannot be set because of the Traffic Separation Lanes. A course of 314°C will cross the eastbound lane at a right angle.** (It should be noted that a Traffic Separation Lane should be crossed as nearly as practicable at right angles to the general direction of the traffic flow. In addition any vessel proceeding under sail at less than 3 knots must use her engine).
use her engine).

B.2   (a) **See plot** on Fig TB1 opposite. The 0700 position can be obtained by using the transferred position line from 0640.

(b) **The 0700 position corresponds well with the EP** using the tidal streams for tidal diamonds Q and P interpolated between Spring and Neap tides.

*Estimation of tidal streams at tidal diamonds P and Q.*

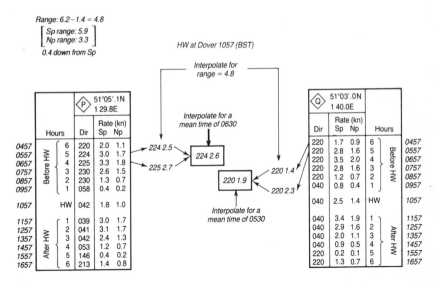

(c) The course for the east entrance of Dover Harbour is **352°C**.

B.3   (a) **Recheck the boat's position, and watch carefully any passing shipping** to see whether any other boat is on a collision or near collision course. **Hoist radar reflector, detail look outs, check foghorn** and **don lifejackets** (uninflated for the moment).

(b) **Apart from shipping, no particular navigational hazards exist**, but should the visibility drop further the boat should not proceed into a water depth of less than 10m until the outer harbour entrance has been located.

B.4 **This is a second trace echo.** Change the echo sounder scale to the next highest range, which should then show a reading of 23m which agrees with the depth on the chart.

B.5 **Port entry signals are found either in Sailing Directions (pilots), or some almanacs.** This particular signal **prohibits entry** to the outer harbour, so watch out for large boats leaving and wait for the signal to be lowered.

B.6 (a)

|        | HW       |        | LW       |        |
|--------|----------|--------|----------|--------|
|        | time     | height | time     | height |
| Dover  | 1057 BST | 6·2m   | 1809 BST | 1·2m   |

Range = 5·0m (0·3 from Springs)
Height of tide 3·7m
At 0827 depth of water below CD is 4·8m −3·7m = 1·1m
Maximum depth is 6·2m + 1·1m = 7·3m (HW height + CD)
Length of chain veered = **22m** (3 × 7·3m)
(b) Depth of LW is 1·2 + 1·1 = 2·3m (LW height + CD)
Draught of boat = 1·9m
Minimum clearance is 2·3m −1·9m = **0·4m**.

# Sailing Terms for the Competent Crew/Day Skipper

## Nautical Terms

**Anchor Roller** A roller over which the anchor chain is passed when at anchor.

**Batten** A flat piece of wood, tufnol or GRP fitted into a pocket on the mainsail to stiffen the leech. Some mainsails are specially cut for use without battens.

**Batten Pocket** A pocket in the sail to hold the batten.

**Bear Away** To alter course away from the direction of the wind.

**Belay** To make fast to a cleat or bollard.

**Boom** A spar which supports the foot of the sail.

**Block** A pulley made of wood, metal or other material.

**Broad Reaching** Sailing with the wind between reaching and running.

**Casting Off** Letting go the warps before leaving a pontoon or berth.

**Cleat** A fitting of tufnol, wood or metal around which a sheet or halyard is fastened (belayed).

**Clew Outhaul** A length of cord or wire attached to the outer end (clew) of the mainsail and the after end of the boom, used for tensioning the foot of the sail (may also be metal jaws running on a track).

**Close Hauled** Sailing as close to the wind as possible with the sheets hauled aft and all sails drawing.

**Close Reaching (Fine Reaching)** Sailing with the wind between close hauled and reaching.

**Coming Alongside** Bringing the boat alongside a pontoon or berth.

**Fairlead** A fitting through which a rope or chain is led, to give a fair lead to a winch, cleat, sail, or anchor, or to prevent chafing.

**Foresail** A sail set immediately before the mast.

**Furling** Stowing a sail on its boom by means of folding or flaking, and then lashing with sail ties. A foresail may also be rolled round a rotating stay.

**Genoa** A large staysail.

**Going About** The action of changing course when the wind is ahead, by steering the boat through the wind.

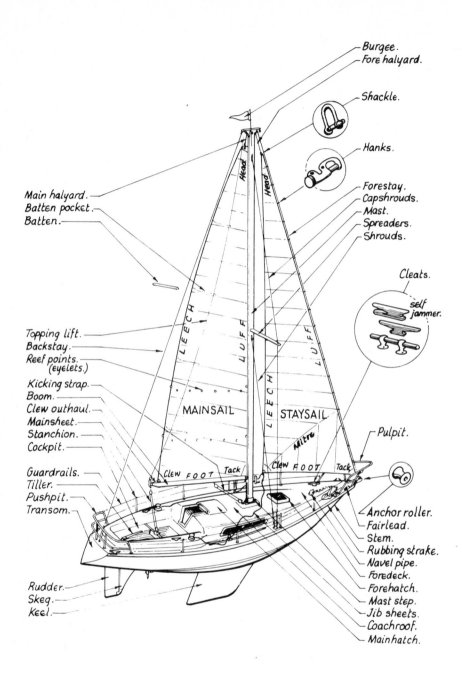

**Fig C1** Parts of the boat and rig.

**Gooseneck** A universal joint fitting on the mast to which the boom is secured.

**Goosewing** To set the foresail and mainsail on opposite sides when running before the wind.

**Guardrail** A length of wire between the pulpit and pushpit, and running through or joined to the stanchions.

**Gybing** To alter course with the wind astern, so that the stern goes through the wind and the boom passes from one side to the other.

**Halyard** A rope or wire attached to the head of a sail for hoisting and lowering.

**Heave-to** A boat is hove-to when the foresail is backed (on the opposite side to the mainsail), as close to the wind as possible. The forward speed is very slow, but in rough weather any violent motion is much reduced.

**In Irons** When the boat loses way head to wind and will not pay off on either tack.

**Jib** A foresail set before the staysail.

**Jib Hanks, Hanks or Piston Hanks** Clips for securing a foresail to a stay.

**Keel** The heavy length of metal projecting below the bottom of the boat, which may be sheathed in plastic. It aids stability and prevents movement of the boat bodily sideways.

**Kicking Strap (Boom Vang)** A rope or tackle to exert a downward pull on the boom to aid the adjustment of the shape of the mainsail.

**Leeward** The opposite side of the boat to that towards which the wind is blowing.

**Luff** To alter course towards the direction of the wind; also the leading edge of a sail.

**Mainsail** The sail set behind the main mast, the luff of which is supported by the mast.

**Mast** A spar which supports the head and the leading edge of the mainsail, and to which the foresails are hoisted.

**Miss Stays** When the boat will not tack through the wind and pays off on the same tack.

**Navel Pipe** A fitting or a hole in the foredeck, through which the anchor chain goes into the chain locker.

**Pinch** To sail continually too close to the wind so that the sails are not properly filled and the boat loses way.

**Pulpit/Pushpit** Rails at the bow/stern of the boat to prevent people falling overboard.

**Reaching** Sailing with the wind on the beam.

**Reefing** Reducing the sail area.

**Reef Points** Short lengths of line secured through a sail above its foot, used for reefing the sail.

**Riding Turn** This occurs when the turns of the sheet around the winch drum become crossed and jam.

**Rudder** A blade for steering the boat. It is pivoted using pins (pintle and gudgeon) or a full length stern post into a guide.

**Running** Sailing with the wind aft.

**Running By The Lee** When on a run and the wind blows over the stern from the same side as the mainsail.

**Running Rigging** The rigging which is not standing, i.e. is adjustable such as: sheets, halyards, kicking strap.

**Samson Post** A strong post on the foredeck to which is secured the anchor chain or warp.

**Sheet** A rope attached to the clew of the sail by which the sail is trimmed as required; it is named after the sail to which it is attached, for example: genoa sheet.

**Sheet Winch** A drum around which the sheets are turned to pull in and ease out the sails; may be geared to give mechanical advantage.

**Shrouds** These are similar to stays, but support the mast in the athwartship position.

**Spinnaker** A large balloon shaped sail hoisted forward of the forestay when reaching or running.

**Spreaders** Struts on the mast which brace the shrouds.

**Stanchions** Upright metal posts along the edge of the deck to which the guardrails are attached.

**Standing Rigging** Galvanised or stainless steel permanent wires supporting the mast, may sometimes be in the form of a stainless steel rod, such as the stays and shrouds. These are attached to the mast at the top or near the spreaders by a pin or shackle, and at the bottom by lashings, a pin or turnbuckles.

**Stays (Backstay/forestay)** Wires supporting the mast in the fore and aft position.

**Staysail** A triangular sail immediately forward of the mast, the luff of which is supported by the forestay.

**Stem** The foremost vertical part of the boat.

**Storm Jib** A very small foresail for heavy weather.

**Storm Trysail** A small strong sail set without a boom in heavy weather, in lieu of the mainsail.

**Tack** To make a course either side of the wind. The tack is defined by the side over which the main boom is carried. Boom over port side, starboard tack; boom over starboard side, port tack. Also the lower forward corner of a sail.

**Tackle** A mechanical device consisting of a rope rove through two or more blocks to increase the purchase of an applied pull.

**Tacking** Making a course to windward by going about, also known as beating or working to windward.

**Tiller** A lever which fits into the rudder for steering.

**Topping Lift** A wire or rope attached to the after end of the boom via a

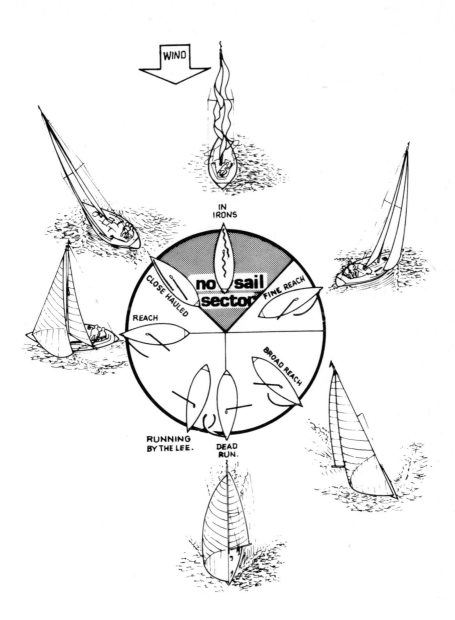

**Fig C2** Points of sailing.

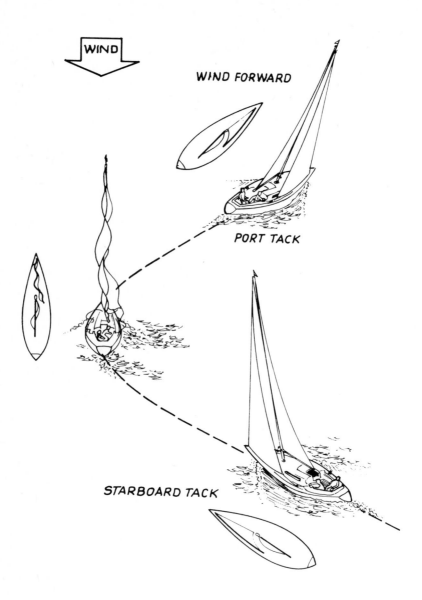

**Fig C3** Going about.

sheave (roller) at the top of the mast. It is used to support the boom when the mainsail is not hoisted.

**To Weather** A boat weathers an object by passing to windward of it. An object which is on the windward side of the boat is said to be up to weather.

**Transom** The transverse flat section at the back of the boat.

**Turnbuckle (Bottlescrew)** A fitting for securing the stays or shrouds to the deck, consisting of a sleeve with a right-handed screw at one end and a left-handed screw at the other end. Sometimes called a rigging screw.

**Under Way** When the boat is not secured in any way to the land.

**Veer** To let out rope or chain as when lowering the anchor. If applied to the wind, when the wind direction alters in a clockwise direction.

**Weighing Anchor** To raise and secure the anchor.

**Windward** The side of the boat towards which the wind is blowing.

## Ropes

Man-made fibre ropes are of three different types of material:

**Nylon** This stretches, so it is ideal for anchor warps or mooring warps.

**Polyester (Terylene)** This stretches much less than nylon and is suitable (particularly in plaited form) for sheets and halyards. Some versions are pre-stretched which are particularly good for halyards. By far the most common rope used for sailing.

**Polypropylene** A buoyant rope which is lightweight, and so it can be used to attach to a lifebuoy.

All ropes, whether natural or man-made fibre, are subject to chafe. Sheets should be led over rollers, and warps protected by passing them through a length of hose, or wrapping a rag around them at the point where they go through the fairlead.

Man-made fibres are rot-proof, but should be washed periodically in fresh water to remove any grit or salt which may have worked its way into the rope and can cause damage. They can be damaged by chemicals and heat.

Ropes are supplied laid up either with three strands, plaited or braided. The stranded version is usually laid up right handed and is coiled in a clockwise direction. Stranded ropes can be spliced, but braided or plaited ones require special tools and techniques.

When securing a rope to a cleat, a round turn is used followed by two or three figure of eight turns, and finished with a round turn which is jammed behind the figure of eight turns. Normally a locking turn is not used when securing a halyard as it may tighten so that the halyard cannot be let off in a hurry. After securing a halyard, the remaining rope is coiled and hung over the cleat or wedged behind the halyard.

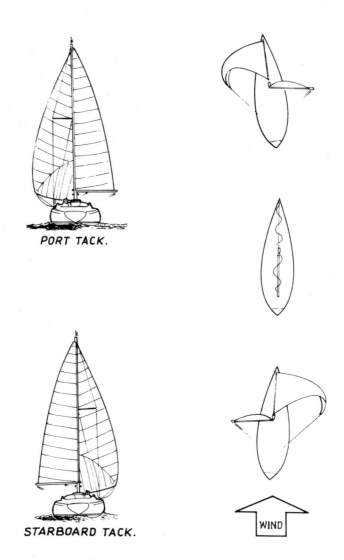

**Fig C4** Gybing.

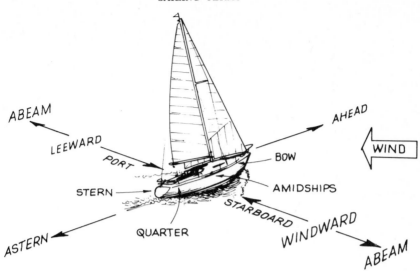

**Fig C5** Sea terms.

Always make sure a rope led to a winch does not develop a riding turn.

On larger boats wire ropes with fibre tails may be used for halyards, in which case *all* the wire must be wound round the winch drum, as to attempt to cleat it would cause kinks.

## Knots

### REEF KNOT

Used for joining two ropes of equal size when bound round an object, e.g. when reefing sails, binding bundles.

**Fig C6** Cleating a rope. A round turn followed by 2 or 3 figure of eight turns, finished by a round turn jammed behind the figure of eight turns.

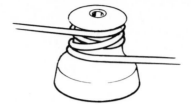

**Fig C7** A riding turn, which can sometimes develop if too many turns of rope are put round the winch when getting the sheet in, or if not enough tension is kept on the rope whilst winching in, or if the lead is wrong.

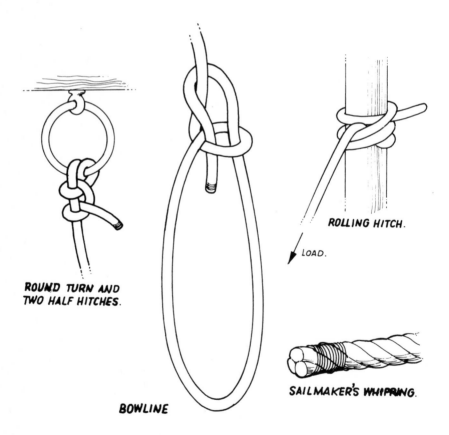

ROUND TURN AND
TWO HALF HITCHES.

BOWLINE

ROLLING HITCH.

LOAD.

SAILMAKER'S WHIPPING.

**Fig C8** Knots you must know how to tie.

FIGURE OF EIGHT

Used to prevent a rope pulling out of a block or an eye, e.g. the free end of a sheet.

CLOVE HITCH

Used to secure a rope to a spar or rail. It is an insecure knot as it can slip along a rail and come undone. Example: two clove hitches tied in the bight of a rope to attach the burgee halyard to the burgee pole.

ROLLING HITCH

Used to secure a rope to a spar or another rope under strain, when the pull is expected to be from one side. Example: taking the strain on a sheet or another warp whilst transferring the lead (the direction in which it is secured).

ROUND TURN AND TWO HALF HITCHES

Used for securing a heavy load to a spar, mooring ring or shackle. It will never jam and can be cast off quickly. Examples: mooring warps, securing a fender to a stanchion.

FISHERMAN'S BEND

Used for attaching a rope to an anchor. It is not easy to undo after a heavy load has been applied.

SHEET BEND

Used to secure a rope's end to an eye or loop, and to attach one rope to another. The double sheet bend should be used for ropes of man-made fibre and of different diameter.

BOWLINE

Used for making a temporary eye or loop in a rope, for example a lifeline around a man's waist. This is a most important useful knot and should be mastered by the competent crew.

MOUSING

A length of line or small wire rove through the eye in a shackle pin or through a turnbuckle to prevent the shackle pin or the turnbuckle from turning, or between the point and shank of a hook to prevent unhooking.

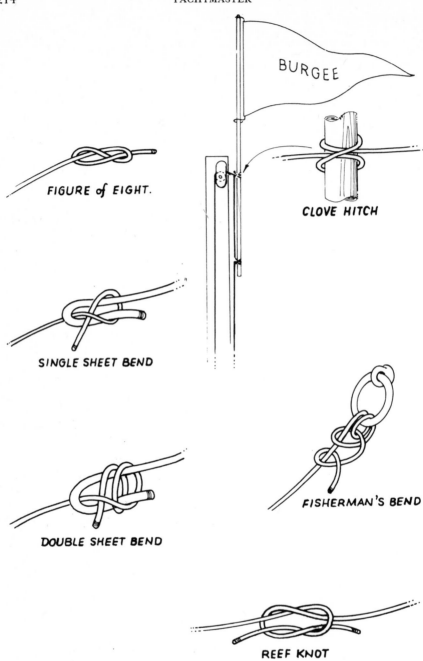

FIGURE of EIGHT.

BURGEE

CLOVE HITCH

SINGLE SHEET BEND

DOUBLE SHEET BEND

FISHERMAN'S BEND

REEF KNOT

**Fig C9** More knots you must know.

# Whippings

COMMON

Used to tie in the strands at the end of a rope which has been cut.

WEST COUNTRY

The same uses as a common whipping but more secure. Useful if it is required to whip the bight of a rope.

SAILMAKERS

A most secure whipping for cable laid rope. It should be used for man-made fibre cordage.

# Splices

BACK SPLICE

An alternative to a whipping for finishing the end of a rope which is not required to be rove through a block.

EYE SPLICE

For making a permanent eye in the end of a rope.

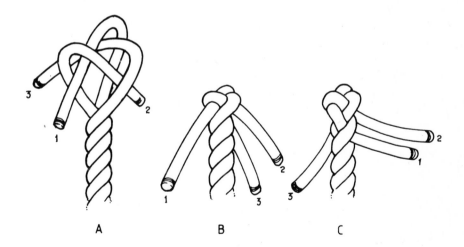

**Fig C10** Back splice. A crown knot is made (A) and pulled tight (B), and then each strand is tucked over the strand in front of it (C) and under the next one (in the standing part); repeat 3 times.

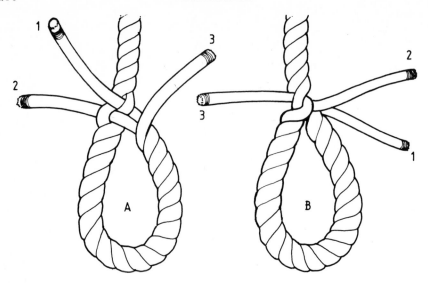

**Fig C11** Eye Splice.
A: strand 1 is tucked under the chosen strand in the standing part. Strand 2 is tucked under the next strand to the left.
B: The splice is turned over. Strand 3 is tucked to the left of strand 2.

When splicing man-made fibres, the strands of the rope are normally fused using heat. Sticky tape can be used to prevent the rope uncoiling further than intended. A permanent eye splice or back splice may be further protected by a whipping or binding with tape.

## Lead Line

The lead line is a useful standby in case of instrument failure. Until the introduction of metrication it has been marked in fathoms, but it is now convenient to use metric markings as shown below:

1 metre  – A piece of leather
2 metres – Two pieces of leather
3 metres – Blue cloth
4 metres – Green and white cloth
5 metres – White cloth
6 metres – Green cloth
7 metres – Red cloth
8 metres – Blue and white cloth
9 metres – Red and white cloth
10 metres – A piece of leather with a hole in it
20 metres – A piece of leather with a hole in it and two leather strips.

11 to 19 metres are the same markings as 1 to 9 metres.

**Note**

The following pages can be used as an index to this book. Find the relevant subject section, and then refer to the page number given in the right hand column.

# Coastal Skipper and Yachtmaster Offshore Syllabus

**SHOREBASED COURSE FOR THE RYA/DoT COASTAL SKIPPER AND YACHTMASTER OFFSHORE CERTIFICATES**

| Item | Subject | Broad detail to be covered | Page |
|------|---------|---------------------------|------|
| 1 | Definition of Position Course and Speed | 1  Latitude and Longitude | 4, 11—14, 18 |
|  |  | 2  Knowledge of standard navigational terms | 18-23 |
|  |  | 3  True bearings and courses | 31 |
|  |  | 4  The knot | 15 |
| 2 | Navigational drawing instruments | 1  Parallel rulers | 5, 18—19 |
|  |  | 2  Dividers and compasses | 5, 18 |
|  |  | 3  Proprietary plotting instruments | 6 |
| 3 | Navigational charts and publications | 1  Suppliers – Admiralty, Stanford, etc. | 1 |
|  |  | 2  Information shown on Admiralty charts | 4 |
|  |  | 3  Chart symbols – Chart 5011 | 7 |
|  |  | 4  Standard Chartwork | 19 |
|  |  | 5  Projections – Mercator and gnomonic | 14,16 |
|  |  | 6  Navigational publications in common use | 6, 7, 225 |
|  |  | 7  Chart correction | 3 |
| 4 | Dead reckoning and Estimated Position | 1  Definition of D.R. and E.P. | 35 |
|  |  | 2.  Working up D.R. and E.P. by plotting on a chart | 40–43 |
| 5 | The position line | 1  Sources of position lines | 48, 50 |
| 6 | The magnetic compass | 1  Allowance for variation. Change of variation with time and position | 27 |
|  |  | 2  Siting of compass and causes of deviation | 30, 35 |
|  |  | 3  Deviation. Allowance for | 30 |
|  |  | 4  Steering and hand bearing compasses | 25, 35 |

# Competent Crew and Day Skipper/Watch Leader Syllabus

**SHOREBASED COURSE FOR THE COMPETENT CREW AND DAY SKIPPER/WATCHLEADER CERTIFICATE**

### Part A Seamanship

| Item | Subject | | Broad Detail to be Covered | Page |
|------|---------|---|---------------------------|------|
| 1 | Nautical terms | 1 | Parts of a boat, hull, rig and sails | 204 |
| | | 2 | General Nautical terminology | |
| | | | | 203, 207–8, 210–11 |
| 2 | Ropework | 1 | Knowledge of the properties of synthetic ropes in common use. | 209 |
| | | 2 | Ability to make, and knowledge of the use of: | 215 |
| | | | figure of eight knot, clove hitch, rolling hitch, reef knot, bowline, single and double sheet bend, round turn and two half hitches, eye splice, common whipping, sail-makers whipping. | 211 |
| | | 3 | Securing to cleats, use of winches and general rope handling. | 211–12 |
| 3 | Anchorwork | 1 | Characteristics of different types of anchor. | 99 |
| | | 2 | Consideration to be taken into account when anchoring. | 106 |
| 4 | Safety | 1 | Knowledge of the safety equipment to be carried, its stowage and use. (RYA booklet G9). | 138 |
| | | 2 | Fire precautions and fire fighting. | 141 |
| | | 3 | Use of personal safety equipment, harnesses and lifejackets. | 134 |
| | | 4 | Ability to send a VHF radio distress message | 129 |

222

| Item | Subject | Broad Detail to be Covered | Page |
|------|---------|----------------------------|------|
| 5 | International Regulations for Preventing Collisions at Sea | 1 Steering and sailing rules (5, 7, 9 & 12–19).<br>2 General rules (all other rules). | 158–65 |

## Part B Navigation and Meteorology

| Item | Subject | Broad Detail to be Covered | Page |
|------|---------|----------------------------|------|
| 6 | Navigational Charts and Publications | 1 Information shown on charts, chart symbols, representation of direction and distance.<br>2 Navigational publications in common use.<br>3 Chart correction. | 4, 15, 19<br>7, 9<br>3 |
| 7 | Navigational drawing instruments | 1 Use of parallel rulers, dividers and proprietary plotting instruments. | 6, 18–19 |
| 8 | Compasses | 1 Application of variation and deviation, and use of transits and comparison to check deviation.<br>2 Importance of swinging compass.<br>3 Use of hand bearing compass.<br>4 Siting of steering compass. | 27, 30, 33<br>32<br>35<br>35 |
| 9 | Chartwork | 1 Working up position from course steered, distance run and estimates of leeway and set.<br>2 Plotting fixes.<br>3 Working out course to steer to allow for leeway and set. | 39<br>49<br>45 |
| 10 | Position Fixing | 1 Sources of position lines.<br>2 Potential accuracy of fixing methods. | 49<br>49, 50, 52 |
| 11 | Tides and tidal streams | 1 Tidal definitions, levels and datums.<br>2 Tide tables, standard and secondary ports.<br>3 Use of the rule of twelfths.<br>4 Tidal stream predictions. | 63, 73<br>66, 69<br>65<br>4 |

| Item | Subject | Broad Detail to be Covered | Page |
|------|---------|---------------------------|------|
| 12 | Pilotage | 1   Use of transits, leading lines and clearing lines. | 50, 53 |
|    |          | 2   IALA system of buoyage for Region A. | 110 |
|    |          | 3   Use of sailing directions. | 7 |
| 13 | Visual aids to navigation | 1   Lighthouses and beacons, light characteristics. | 7, 116–7 |
| 14 | Passage planning | 1   Preparation of navigational plan for short coastal passages | 170 |
| 15 | Navigation in Restricted Visibility | 1   Precautions to be taken and limitations imposed by fog. | 151–2 |
| 16 | Meteorology | 1   Sources of broadcast meteorological information. | 86 |
|    |          | 2   Knowledge of terms used in shipping forecasts, including the Beaufort Scale, and their significance to small craft. | 90–3 |

# Bibliography

*Reed's Nautical Almanac* (Thomas Reed Publications Ltd)
*Channel West and Solent Almanac* (Adlard Coles Ltd)

*Admiralty Tide Tables* (Hydrographic Department)
*Admiralty Tidal Atlas* (Hydrographic Department)

RYA Publications
*G16 Safety Boat Handbook*
*G2 IRPCS*

*Normandy Harbours and Pilotage* (Brackenbury) (Adlard Coles Limited)
*North Brittany Pilot* (RCC Pilotage Foundation) (Adlard Coles Limited)
*North Biscay Pilot* (RCC Pilotage Foundation) (Adlard Coles Limited)
*South Biscay Pilot* (Brandon) (Adlard Coles Limited)

*Radio Position Fixing for Yachtsmen* (Claud Powell) (Adlard Coles Ltd)
*VHF Yachtmaster* (Pat Langley-Price and Philip Ouvry) (Adlard Coles Ltd)
*Yachtmaster Exercises* (Pat Langley-Price and Philip Ouvry) (Adlard Coles Ltd)

# International Code of Signals

| FLAG | PHONETIC ALPHABET<br>MORSE<br>MEANING OF LETTER<br>(signalled by any means) |
|------|------|

 **Alfa**
• ▬

I have a diver down;
keep well clear at slow
speed.

 **Bravo**
▬ • • •

I am taking in, or
discharging, or carrying
dangerous goods.

 **Charlie**
▬ • ▬ •

Yes

 **Delta**
▬ • •

Keep clear of me; I am
manoeuvring with
difficulty.

 **Echo**
•

I am altering my course
to starboard.

 **Foxtrot**
• • ▬ •

I am disabled;
communicate with me.

 **Golf**
▬ ▬ •

I require a pilot.

 **Hotel**
• • • •

I have a pilot on board.

 **India**
• •

I am altering my course
to port.

 **Juliett**
• ▬ ▬ ▬

I am on fire and have
dangerous cargo on board;
keep well clear of me.

 **Kilo**
▬ • ▬

I wish to communicate
with you.

 **Lima**
• ▬ • •

You should stop your
vessel instantly.

 **Mike**
▬ ▬

My vessel is stopped and
making no way through
the water.

 **November**
▬ •

No.

 **Oscar**
▬ ▬ ▬

Man overboard.

 **Papa**
• ▬ ▬ •

*In harbour.* All persons
should report aboard as
the vessel is about to
proceed to sea.
*At sea.* My nets have
come fast upon an
obstruction (used by
fishing vessels).

 **Quebec**
▬ ▬ • ▬

My vessel is healthy and I
request free pratique.

 **Romeo**
• ▬ •

No meaning in the Flag
Code, but morse signal
used by vessels at anchor
to warn of danger of
collision in fog.